the essential

pie cookbook

Dark
Chocolate
Pecan Pie
page 69

# the essential pie cookbook

## 50 Sweet & Savory Recipes

**Edited by Saura Kline**

**Cover Photography by Andrew Purcell**

ROCKRIDGE
PRESS

I dedicate this book to my Aunt Mary and Uncle Bruce, whose love and support throughout my life has allowed me to be where I am today.

For general information on our other products and services or to obtain technical support, please contact our Customer Care Department within the United States at (866) 744-2665, or outside the United States at (510) 253-0500.

Rockridge Press publishes its books in a variety of electronic and print formats. Some content that appears in print may not be available in electronic books, and vice versa.

TRADEMARKS: Rockridge Press and the Rockridge Press logo are trademarks or registered trademarks of Callisto Media Inc. and/or its affiliates, in the United States and other countries, and may not be used without written permission. All other trademarks are the property of their respective owners. Rockridge Press is not associated with any product or vendor mentioned in this book.

Interior and Cover Designer: Angie Chiu
Art Producer: Janice Ackerman
Editor: Cecily McAndrews

Photography: ii–iii: ©Annie Martin (background image) & Marija Vidal (pie images); viii: ©Antonis Achilleos; vi: ©Darren Muir; pp. 9–11: ©Darren Muir; pp. 13–15: ©Darren Muir; p. 20: ©Darren Muir; p. 32: ©Darren Muir; p. 36: © Darren Muir; p. 40: ©Darren Muir; p. 42: ©Darren Muir; p. 47: ©Laura Flippen; p. 55: ©Darren Muir; p. 60: ©Darren Muir; p. 64: ©Darren Muir; p. 68: ©Nadine Greeff; p. 72: ©Darren Muir; p. 78: ©Darren Muir; p. 86: ©Hélène Dujardin; p. 90: ©Emulsion Studio; p. 92: ©Darren Muir; p. 96: ©Darren Muir; p. 101: ©Darren Muir; p. 109: ©Evi Abeler; p. 114: ©Darren Muir; p. 122: ©Darren Muir; p. 126: ©Cayla Zahoran; p. 130: ©Antonis Achilleos; p. 135: ©LauraFlippen; p. 140: ©Cayla Zahoran

ISBN: Print 978-1-63807-071-9
eBook 978-1-63807-823-4
R0

# contents

# introduction

If you're like me, you express love through food. Sharing food is how we make new friends, how we stay connected with old friends, how we celebrate achievements, and how we show our love when there are grievances. Food brings people together after a long day of work or at weekend dinners with friends or family. Food is at the center of any celebrated holiday. Sharing a meal with loved ones is how we stay connected, and the better the food, the better the experience.

I had the greatest feeling of relief when I realized I could turn my extreme passion for food into a career. Fast-forward 15 years and I'm now an executive pastry chef, cookbook author, and dessert blogger. I live, eat, breathe, and sleep desserts. Don't get me wrong, I love to cook other things, too, but dessert is my true passion. And of all the desserts in the world, nothing says love more to me than a homemade pie.

I have my grandmother to thank for that. She was a true homemaker, and on a visit to her house when I was a little girl, she made me a homemade pie using peaches from the tree in her backyard. I fell in love instantly. The juicy sweet peach filling was complemented by the all-butter, flaky homemade crust. I could taste the love in that pie. For years following that experience, I requested a peach pie for my birthday instead of a traditional birthday cake. Not long after that, I realized that I wanted to pursue a career in baking. They say if you love what you do, you'll never work a day in your life. I can attest that statement rings true.

Pies are a staple celebratory food, weekend treat, or even a weeknight meal. They can be sweet, savory, open face, or even handheld. You don't even need a pie dish to make a pie! Pie baking is a labor of love. It can sometimes seem intimidating, but it doesn't have to be. When you break it down, pie is just a crust and filling. You can dress it up if desired, but even a humble pie is top notch, and that's really all that matters.

Different seasons call for different pies. Different events call for different pies. Whether you're making a pie for a loved one or just for a weeknight bake, all you need is a good, solid recipe. That's where this book comes in. These recipes are a collection of great, tried-and-true recipes from various authors. In these pages, you can access not only the best crust recipes but also recipes for fabulous fruit pies, creamy pies, nutty pies, chocolate pies, savory pies, and more. These are the 50 best pie recipes out there. Everyone needs an essential cookbook in their repertoire, and this book is here to serve that purpose. Whatever type of pie you're looking to make, and whether you're new to baking or you've been baking for years, you've come to the right place.

# 1

# Pie: A Love Story

**If** you're reading this, chances are you have a fondness for pie. Hello, fellow pie lover. In this chapter, I'll go over what pie is and all the various types of pie out there. In addition, I'll cover how to read the recipes in this book and how to determine weight versus volume when measuring ingredients. I'll discuss essential pie equipment to ensure you feel completely comfortable baking in your own kitchen. I'll go over common pie baking techniques and how to enhance your pie to make it a showstopper. And last, I'll address some common troubleshooting queries so you can feel confident when you bake your next pie.

# Pies Here, There, and Everywhere

It's all about pie. It's not only the best dessert there is, it's also the best anytime food.

At its simplest, pie is crust and filling. The variety of flavor combinations and textural elements you can put into that crust and filling is what makes pie so amazing. Pie can be sweet, nutty, chocolatey, fruity, or a combination. It can also be savory: consider hearty meat pies, silky pot pies, or even an all-vegetable dish.

You don't even need a pie dish to make a pie. Whether it be a rustic galette, a slab pie to feed a crowd, or a hand pie for a to-go treat, you'll be satisfied no matter which form you choose. As long as it has crust and a filling, well, it's a pie!

# Pie Prep

Like all things in life, it's important to be prepared before starting anything new. Here, I'll discuss some of the ways you can set yourself up for successful baking. As a professionally trained pastry chef, I learned the importance of this early on. In a professional kitchen, it's called *mise en place*. Loosely translated, it means having your stuff ready. This involves making sure you have all the ingredients, prepping them ahead of time, and getting all your equipment out of the cupboards and ready for use—essentially, it's about preparing what you need ahead of time, so you can cook or bake with success and less stress. And exactly how do I know what "stuff" to get "ready"? I'm glad you asked!

## Recipe 101

The most important part of any bake is to read the recipe all the way through before you begin. Not only do you want to make sure you have all the ingredients and equipment needed, but also the time needed, so nothing can throw you off your pie game. This is the number one rule that can make all the difference when baking or cooking in general. If you know your pie needs to chill for several hours before you can apply the topping, schedule your time accordingly. You don't want to start making a pie you plan to serve that same day, only to learn halfway through that it needs to be chilled for a duration of time before you can serve it.

## Measuring

Unlike most general cooking, baking requires precision. In any given recipe, the ratio between fat, sugar, eggs, dry, and liquid is set for a reason. To vary from a recipe can sometimes drastically throw it off. If you've had baking experiences where a recipe didn't quite turn out the way it was supposed to, it's likely because the ingredients weren't measured properly. Luckily, there are a few ways to get an accurate measurement.

## DRY INGREDIENTS

Dry ingredients include flour, flour alternatives such as gluten-free flour or almond flour, sugars, salt, spices, leavening ingredients such as baking powder and baking soda, and nuts. To measure these properly, you'll need some trusty measuring cups. A standard set includes ¼ cup, ⅓ cup, ½ cup, ¾ cup, and 1 cup. In addition, you'll need some measuring spoons. These spoons can accurately measure increments of teaspoons and tablespoons. When measuring dry ingredients, here's the best way to do it: To get the proper measurement of 1 cup of flour, scoop the 1-cup measure into the flour. Be careful not to pack it in. Run the flat edge of a butter knife over the top of the measuring cup to sweep any excess flour off the top. Use the same process if using a measuring spoon: Scoop the spoon into the dry ingredient. Be careful not to pack in in. Level the top with a butter knife.

## WET INGREDIENTS

Wet ingredients include milk or milk alternatives, water, cream, stock, and lemon juice. These require a liquid measuring cup. This is a clear cup with markings up the side to indicate the measurement. To properly measure a wet ingredient, fill the cup with the ingredient to the indicated line that you need. You may need to bend down so you can see the marking at eye level, to make sure you've got it to the correct line. Most liquid measuring cups include ¼ cup, ⅓ cup, ½ cup, ⅔ cup, ¾ cup, 1 cup, and sometimes beyond.

## VOLUME AND WEIGHT

Volume measurements are done in measuring cups and spoons, whereas weight measurement is based off a food scale. One cup of flour can weigh a slightly different amount each time you measure it, which is exactly why most professional kitchens rely on weight measurement for accuracy. Don't feel intimidated, however. It's actually quite easy and well worth it to weigh the ingredients. A good food scale can cost $10 to $15, and it's a compact tool that'll fit easily in your kitchen. The pie recipes in this book generally have volume measurements. The crust can be more finicky and for that reason both weight and volume measurements are listed. For your convenience, there's a metric conversion chart on page 141.

## Temperature

Temperature is a factor at every stage of your pie baking experience: The ambient temperature of your kitchen, the temperature of the ingredients, and the temperature of the oven are all important for a successful pie.

Winter cold, summer heat, and humidity can all factor into your bake. Be mindful of them. To combat heat, make sure the necessary ingredients stay cold. To counteract cold weather conditions, you can warm up your kitchen by turning the oven on ahead of time. When it's humid out, sift all dry ingredients thoroughly before use.

Piecrust is particularly vulnerable to temperature. First, always start with very cold butter. Cold butter equals flaky pie dough. If your kitchen is warm, keep that butter in the refrigerator or freezer when it's not in use. After you've made and fitted the dough into a pie dish, chill the piecrust until you're ready to bake. Unless otherwise specified in the recipe, assume that all other ingredients can be used at room temperature. When you're ready to use the oven, make sure it's preheated to the required temperature. If you're waiting for the oven to heat, keep the pie in the refrigerator. It's important to heat the oven properly before you bake. If your oven is still warming up when you put the pie in, the crust won't get the proper heat it needs and can melt before it has a chance to bake.

## Essential Pie Equipment

Every pie baker needs some trusty tools in their arsenal. Here's what you absolutely need to create a great pie, along with some information about how to get by if you don't have access to certain equipment. Each of these tools can be found locally at a houseware store or even your grocery store, as well as on Amazon.

**Pie dishes.** First and foremost, you need some pie dishes. These come in glass, ceramic, and aluminum options. They can range in price; generally, the more decorative it is, the more expensive it is. However, a good tip would be to check out your local thrift store. I've found a lot of great dishes there, each for under $5. I recommend glass and ceramic pie dishes for a couple of reasons. First, both are a standard 9-inch size and fit the recipes in this book perfectly. Aluminum pans are usually a little smaller, so the fillings in this book might overflow. Second, heat holds longer and more evenly in a glass or ceramic dish, so you'll find that your pie has a more even bake.

**Measuring cups.** To create the recipe properly, you'll need liquid and dry measuring cups, and measuring spoons. Measuring cups are inexpensive and range in materials from plastic to copper. Any material you choose is great; they just need to be durable.

**Rolling pin.** To roll out pie dough, you need a trusty rolling pin. Rolling pins are inexpensive and there are a few styles of rolling pins out there: a classic wood rolling pin with handles, a wood French rolling pin, and some plastic or metal ones. A French rolling pin has no handles but rather a tapered edge. All rolling pins work,
so it's more about your personal preference. I prefer a classic wood rolling pin with handles. I find that getting a good grip on the handles gives me the control over the dough that I need. If your pie dough is very firm, handles on the rolling pin give you more leverage.

**Food processor or pastry cutter.** Admittedly, the most difficult aspect to creating a pie is making the piecrust, which is why you need either a food processor or a pastry cutter—either tool makes it easy. Food processors can range in price and features, but they are generally on the more expensive side, ranging from $50 to as much as $200. They range in size from 3 cups to about 12 cups. I use a standard 8-cup (64-ounce) food processor. This

size allows enough room for a double crust pie dough. They are a good investment if you bake or cook often, as they can be helpful for a number of other tasks, too. If you don't have a food processor, a pastry cutter is necessary. Making piecrust is essentially mixing cold butter into dry flour. It requires a sharp tool to help you do this, and a pastry cutter works wonders. It's inexpensive and small enough to fit in a kitchen drawer.

**Pastry brush.** A pastry brush may not seem like much, but if you want a beautiful sheen on your double crust or lattice pies, you'll need a brush to apply an egg wash. They're inexpensive and come in silicone or boar bristles. Both work great.

**Whisk.** This handy tool may be in your kitchen already, but if not, consider getting one. It can be used for everything from whisking a filling together to whipping up some cream to top your pie. A whisk comes in a variety of materials, but I find that a sturdy metal whisk is the best way to go. It's firm and holds up well to any ingredient you're trying to whisk.

## Do I need a stand mixer or food processor?

Although a stand mixer is a convenient, handy piece of equipment to have, it is not essential. You can easily do without one. If a recipe calls for a stand mixer, you can use an electric hand mixer or even just a whisk. It's important to note, however, that the speed and time of making the pie will vary when using a stand mixer versus an electric hand mixer versus a whisk. You can take cues for readiness from what you're mixing. If it's whipped cream, watch the texture of the cream. See how it goes from soft peaks to stiff, and be careful not to overwhip it.

Although convenient, a food processor also is not essential. Food processors are typically used to make pie dough or a cookie crust, but a pastry cutter can be used to make pie dough. If you're making a cookie crust, and the recipe calls for you to crumble cookies in a food processor, simply put the required cookies in a large, sturdy, resealable plastic bag, then smash them with a rolling pin. When the cookie crumbs are crushed, pour them into a bowl and mix with melted butter.

## Essential Pie Ingredients

A few ingredients are essential to creating a great pie. Here's what you need to stock your kitchen to be pie-ready.

**Butter.** I'm a sucker for butter. Pure, unadulterated, full-fat butter. I like the texture and the taste, and there's just no substitute. Unsalted butter is always the way to go. Remember, you can always add salt, but you cannot take it away. Unsalted is the standard butter to use for all baking for this reason.

The only reason I'll use anything apart from butter is if I want to give a savory pie some more depth, in which case I'll use a combination of butter and lard. Lard is pure pig fat, so it gives the pie an umami flavor. Because lard is pure fat, the texture is crumbly, so it needs to be combined with either butter or more water.

Shortening is another fat often used by itself or in combination with butter. A lot of people swear by shortening, and it was commonly used in the old days. I cannot get excited about the texture and it has little to no flavor, but if you're a die-hard shortening fan, by all means use it!

**Chocolate.** Chocolate is not quite an essential ingredient, as it is (obviously) used only in chocolate pies. For these occasions, though, keep your pantry stocked with unsweetened cocoa powder and some good-quality chocolate baking bars. When shopping for cocoa powder, I opt for Dutch process cocoa powder. It's darker and I like the flavor better. However, natural cocoa powder will work with any of the recipes in this book as well. Some recipes call for unsweetened chocolate, and some call for dark chocolate. Unsweetened bars are 100 percent chocolate with no added sugar. It typically has a deeper chocolate flavor, which will lead to a great-tasting chocolate pie. Sweetened dark chocolate bars have a lower percentage of cacao (often this is marked on the bar; higher percentage bars are richer tasting but also more bitter) and already contain sugar. These bars are equally good for baking and also are a great snack for the baker.

**Eggs.** Use whole large eggs. Some recipes may use the entire egg, whereas others will call for just the yolks or the whites. It's important to store eggs in the refrigerator to keep them fresh for longer.

**Flour.** All you need is some form of all-purpose flour, either gluten free or regular. I like King Arthur All-Purpose flour because they have high-quality products and they are an employee-owned company. When selecting a gluten-free flour, I look for one that contains xanthan gum in its blend. Xanthan gum is a binding agent that helps the structure of the bake, and most gluten-free recipes call for it. Why spend more money on both xanthan gum and gluten-free flour when you can buy flour that already contains the gum? The brand I use is Bella Gluten-Free, and it can be found online through Amazon, the company's website, and in many grocery stores.

**Leavening.** Leavening ingredients include baking soda and baking powder. Although a leavener is not always found in pie baking, you will see it occasionally. As a baker, you'll want to keep these ingredients stocked in your pantry. Be aware that leavener has an expiration date, so check the package to make sure yours is still fresh.

**Spices.** Some great spices to keep stocked for delicious pies include cinnamon, cardamom, allspice, nutmeg, cloves, and ginger. When shopping for spices, always opt for the ground versions. For optimum freshness, keep the spices tightly sealed when not using.

**Sugar.** Keep a supply of granulated sugar, brown sugar, and powdered sugar in your pantry. These ingredients are essential for sweet pies. Although there are some substitutes, such as stevia, all the sweet recipes in this book use standard sugars.

**Vanilla extract.** Good quality vanilla extract can make a great difference to a bake. Good vanilla tends to be expensive, but only a little is required for each recipe. Make sure your bottle says pure vanilla extract and not imitation vanilla.

## Dietary Substitutions

Sometimes, an ingredient just doesn't work well in our bodies. Whether you opt for gluten-free, nut-free, or dairy-free food, everybody should enjoy the pie they're eating, and there are usually ingredient substitutes that can make that happen. Gluten free is probably the most common need, and I've got a perfect substitute for that: Try the Gluten-Free Crust on page 24. This crust will work with any pie in the book as an easy swap for the wheat-flour standard. You can use this crust recipe interchangeably with the All-Butter Crust (page 22).

If you're unable to consume nuts, no need to worry. There are many nut-free pies in this book, such as Strawberry-Rhubarb Lattice Pie (page 43) or Mudslide Ice Cream Pie (page 120).

Dairy is a common ingredient in the pies in this book; however, in most cases, dairy milk can be substituted with a plant-based milk such as coconut milk or almond milk. Dairy-free butters are more commonly found in grocery stores these days, and that can be a great substitute for dairy butter in piecrust recipes. An important rule for piecrust is to always keep the butter cold, and that applies to dairy-free butters, too.

# Techniques

Every avid pie baker has an arsenal of techniques they've acquired through their years of baking. Whether it's a simple method of freezing the butter, a special way to decorate the edge, or even a combination of ingredients to make the perfect egg wash, those tried-and-true techniques make your pie stand out, and each trick is unique to the baker. Because this book is compiled from multiple authors, you'll see a variety of techniques throughout. I'm here to tell you I've tried them all, and yes, they're all great methods, but it's ultimately your decision as to which methods work best for you.

## Cutting in Butter

Probably the most widely disputed technique in the world of pie baking is cutting in the butter. There are multiple ways to do this and certainly no "right" way. Using a food processor, which is my preferred method and the most convenient way, lets the machine do the work. You simply put in the butter and dry ingredients and turn the machine on Ⓐ! Process until the mixture looks crumbly Ⓑ. Drizzle in ice-cold water until the dough forms Ⓒ. This method cuts the butter into tiny, even pieces so that the butter is evenly distributed throughout the dough.

A pastry cutter is a handheld way to make dough. This method requires an arm workout, but the results show the love that is put into it. Combine cold butter cubes and dry ingredients in a bowl, and start cutting with the pastry cutter. Drizzle in a little ice water at a time and continue to work that pastry cutter until your dough forms. This method yields uneven chunks of butter distributed throughout the dough,

which can in turn result in a flakier crust. Remember, friends: butter chunks = flaky crust.

The same can be said for the two knives version. It's essentially the same method as using a pastry cutter, but instead of a pastry cutter, you use two knives to cut the butter into the dry ingredients.

The last method is grating in the butter. For this method, freeze the butter solid first; that way it won't melt while being grated. Place the dry ingredients in a bowl and use the large holes of a cheese or box grater to grate the ice-cold butter over top. Once it is all grated, pour in ice water, a little at a time, while folding with a rubber spatula, until the dough comes together. This method is similar to the first where the butter chunks are the same size and evenly distributed; it just requires a little more elbow grease.

For all these methods, gather the dough together to form it into a uniform ball . They all yield a great piecrust, some a little flakier than others. The technique that works the best for you is the one you should stick with.

## Rolling Dough

When rolling out pie dough, make sure to do so on a clean, dry surface. Follow these simple instructions to roll out your pie like a pro:

1. Lightly flour the work surface and rolling pin with some flour. Unwrap the dough onto the floured surface .

2. Use the rolling pin to begin to roll the dough from the center outward. Turn the dough 90 degrees and roll

again from the center out. Continue to roll and turn to get the dough rolled even and uniformly into the required size **F**.

For a standard 9-inch pie plate, roll the dough into a roughly 16-inch-diameter circle. For a slab pie, roll the dough into a rectangular shape, about 11 by 16 inches. For a galette, roll the dough into a 16-inch-diameter circle. If cracks appear or pieces get torn off while rolling, simply patch the dough back together, no harm, no foul.

## Transferring Dough to a Pie Plate

The best way to get rolled-out dough into a pie plate is actually easier than it seems. Don't fuss over lifting each edge at the same time; instead, follow these simple steps to transfer dough to a pie plate with ease.

1. Starting from the edge of the dough, roll it up on the rolling pin as if you were rolling up a piece of paper **G**.

2. Move the rolling pin over the top of the pie dish and simply unroll the dough onto the pie dish **H**.

3. Press the dough around the edge and into every crevice of the dish **I**.

4. Trim and crimp the edge as desired. Easy, right?

For a slab pie, use the same method of rolling the dough onto the rolling pin and off onto a 10-by-15-inch jelly-roll pan, and trim the sides. For a galette, roll the dough onto the rolling pin, then off onto a parchment-lined baking sheet. After transferring the dough to a pie dish, remember to keep the pie dough in the refrigerator while you prepare the filling.

## Fluting Edges/Decorating

The way you flute your pie is purely decorative, so it isn't going to affect the final taste in any way. However, it can give your pie a truly "finished" look. You can do the scalloped technique, which is where you pinch the edge around your index finger. This is my go-to flute technique and it's quite simple to do. Another way is to use a fork to indent marks alongside the edge, and it's probably the easiest. I'll go over more design techniques in the next section.

## Washes

What sort of wash to use varies from baker to baker. The most common egg wash is water and a whole egg. It has fat from the yolk, protein from the white, and the water dilutes it just enough to help it spread on the crust. This is a simple way to give a pie surface a nice finish. Want to make it shinier? Use milk. Want to make it darker? Sprinkle on some sugar. Want to make it thicker? Use only yolks. Me, I'm a purist. I use the classic whole egg and water, every time.

## Can I Use a Store-Bought Crust?

There's nothing like the joy and pride that comes from making your own piecrust, but to be honest, we all have lives. And that means sometimes we don't have the time it requires to make a homemade crust. Should we be judged for that? Absolutely not. Store-bought crust is one of those modern luxuries we must all take advantage of when we need to. Maybe there's a school bake sale you found out about last minute, or you've been assigned dessert duty at your company holiday party. Pie baking requires planning. So when you can't budget in the time for a crust, head to your local grocery store and find the rolled-up piecrust in the refrigerated section. I prefer these to the already rolled out frozen piecrust in the freezer aisle. Refrigerated crusts can be unrolled easily into your pie dish at home.

# Pretty Pies

Once you have the basics of pie-making down, the next step in a baker's journey is how to make that pie more aesthetically pleasing. There are several ways you can kick your pretty pie up a notch. There are some classic methods as well as some modern ways you may not have heard of yet.

## Crimping/Fluting Edges

My favorite crimping method is the scalloped edge. It's the method I was taught as a young girl, and it's the same one I do to this day. In fact, when I'm shaping a crust into a pie dish, I'm usually on autopilot, making the same motions I've done for decades, without a thought! The scalloped edge is a classic technique that gives your pie that home-baked look. Place your index finger on one side of the crust and pinch the dough around that finger on the other side. Continue this around the entire edge of the pie. A fun way I like to enhance this is to exaggerate the scallops a bit, to give the pie a dramatic flair. To do this, you'll want to bulk up the sides of the crust a bit with extra dough. Then indent each scallop about ¾ to 1 inch, to get a really nice dramatic border.

## Lattice Top

Ah, the lattice top. If you close your eyes and picture the quintessential pie cooling on a windowsill, I bet it has a lattice top. Fortunately, making a lattice is a lot easier than you might think. To get started, roll out the dough as usual, then cut it into 10 (1-inch) strips **A**. Place 5 dough strips horizontally across the top of the pie, about 1 inch apart **B**. Pull back 3 alternate strips to the center and lay down 1 strip vertically **C**. Replace the horizontal pieces **D**. Pull the other 2 horizontal strips toward the center, stopping at the first vertical strip **E**. Position another vertical strip; replace the 2 horizontal pieces **F**. Repeat with the first 3 horizontal strips to finish one side of the pie. Repeat the process on the other side until the lattice covers the top of the pie. Seal and crimp as desired. Et voila! Once you get the hang of a simple lattice, you can enhance your design with braid work by replacing one strip of dough with a braid of dough. Another way to enhance this design is to use a fluted pastry cutter to cut the strips of dough. So easy and so pretty!

## Cutout Tops

Pie decorating is evolving, and often you'll see pies with a cutout scene of beautiful floral shapes, leaves, stars, or more. This technique involves a top crust and an X-Acto knife. It is quickly becoming a new pie decorating trend. When using a top crust, trace cutout edges with the knife to cut out a shape. This can be done by printing out an image and replicating that image on a top crust before applying that crust to the pie.

## Other Easy Edges

One of my new favorite edges is a braided edge. For this technique, use the dough for a top crust, and roll it out into a thin rectangle. Then cut three thin strips and use them to make a long braid. Apply the braid to the edge of the crust with some egg wash to stick.

## Leftover Crust Cookies/Chips

Use cookie cutters to add cute embellishments to your pie. This technique is fun to do around holidays, because you can decorate the pie to match that holiday. This can be done a couple different ways.

1.  Use cookie cutters on leftover pie dough to cut out shapes. Sprinkle with cinnamon sugar and bake at 350°F until golden brown. Once cooled, you can use the cookie shapes to garnish a custard pie.

2.  Use pieces of leftover dough cut with cookie cutters to embellish a lattice-top pie. I like to place them around the edge before baking.

3.  Use a cookie cutter to punch out all the dough of an entire top crust. Use those cutouts to completely top a pie. My favorite cookie cutter shape to use for pies are leaves. They give a nice fall look for holiday pies. You can find various types of leaf shapes on Amazon or in your local craft store.

## Forming Hand Pies and Toaster Pastries

The classic toaster pastry is an easy rectangle shape. These are two rectangles and can be cut out using a knife and ruler. You could also use a large circular, square, oval, or even a heart cookie cutter. The same method applies: Place the filling in the center of one piece of dough, leaving the outer rim clean. Top the filling with the second piece of dough and crimp the edges with a fork to seal.

## Go-To Galettes

Don't own a pie dish? Not to worry; go for a galette! This rustic pie is incredibly easy and just as impressive. Essentially, *galette* is the French term for a free-form pie that is baked flat on a baking sheet (you might also know this by its Italian name, *crostata,* which are typically made with fruits and nuts). Almost any pie can be turned into a galette, with the exception of cream or custard pies. It has the same beginnings as any pie, by first making a piecrust. Roll out the dough, transfer it to a baking sheet, top the center with filling, and crimp the sides over the filling. A quick egg wash and a bake is all that's left before you're able to feast. Check out some great galettes in this book, such as Summer Peach Galette (page 45), or Asparagus, Spinach, and Parmesan Galette with Sunny-Side-Up Eggs (page 97).

## Troubleshooting/FAQs

Baking provides a sense of peace for me; it's my happy place. It's probably why I chose that path as a career. I usually thoroughly enjoy every moment, except on those occasions when I'm having baking issues I can't get past. If you're in that same boat, I've got you covered. Here are some common pie troubleshooting tips to get you back into your baking zen.

### How do I avoid soggy bottoms?

If you've struggled with soggy bottoms before, try this tip: Use a pizza stone, or just invert a baking sheet upside down and place it on the center rack of the oven. Let it heat up with the oven completely, about 30 minutes, before putting in the pie. Put the pie on the hot stone or baking sheet, and bake for the time indicated in the recipe. The pizza stone will conduct heat to the bottom while the oven bakes the pie.

**Why is there a gap between my filling and top crust?**

The gap occurs because there is not enough starch to keep the filling from deflating during the bake. When a pie bakes, it heats up, which causes the filling to expand. If there is not enough starch in the recipe, it will just deflate after it's baked and cooled. Add 1 to 2 more tablespoons of cornstarch or flour to the filling recipe.

**Why did my custard crack in the oven?**

A custard will crack during the bake for two reasons: it's been baked too long, or the oven temperature is too high. Try turning down the oven by 25 degrees or baking for 5 minutes less.

**Why is my crust turning too dark before the filling is done?**

Some ovens run hotter than others. A piecrust shield is a popular tool that can prevent a crust browning too fast. Place the piecrust shield over the pie for the first 20 minutes of the bake. Remove the shield and continue to bake as directed in the instructions. If you don't have a piecrust shield, substitute with a piece of aluminum foil.

# About the Recipes

What really makes a great pie is the love you bake it with. And in this book, you have a compilation of recipes to guide your baking. Throughout these pages, you'll find some quintessential, classic flavors in all categories. These are tried-and-true recipes that have graced holiday and family tables for years. You'll also find some not-so-traditional pie recipes that might never have been in your grandma's recipe box, but they're yours now, and maybe in the future, they'll be your grandchildren's favorites.

With the basics of pie baking covered, it's time to get ready to bake. Throughout the following chapters, you'll find every pie imaginable, and even better, every crust option you could ever want. My favorite crust, the All-Butter Crust, is on page 22. Most of the pies in this book will use the crusts presented in chapter 2.

Whether it be a sweet or savory pie, all the pies in this book list ingredients that are easily accessible year-round at most grocery stores. Furthermore, each recipe works great for any time of the year. Sure, everyone has their favorite seasonal pies, but I urge you to flip through these pages and see if a new pie stands out to you.

All-Butter
Crust
page 22

# Crusts

# All-Butter Crust

Makes 1 (9-inch)
single crust
standard pie or
deep-dish pie

Prep time:
10 minutes, plus
30 minutes to chill

Bake time:
20 minutes (par-
tial blind bake) or
35 minutes (full
blind bake)

Look no further for the ultimate piecrust. This all-butter recipe is tried and true, and the most universal. It can be used with sweet or savory fillings, for hand pies or slab pies, and for single or double crusts. This crust easily fits in a standard or deep-dish pie dish, and when doubled yields just a little extra to use for design pieces. It's my favorite crust to use for most pies; the texture is just the right amount of flaky and tender you want in a piecrust.

8 tablespoons (1 stick; 113 grams) cold unsalted butter

1¼ cups (160 grams) all-purpose flour

1½ teaspoons granulated sugar

¼ teaspoon salt

2 to 3 tablespoons ice water

1. Cut the butter into small cubes. Place them in a large metal bowl and put the bowl in the freezer until needed.

2. In a food processor, pulse the flour, sugar, and salt to combine. Add the chilled butter cubes and process for 30 seconds until the mixture looks like dry crumbles. Add 1 tablespoon of ice water and process for 20 seconds. Continue adding ice water, 1 tablespoon at a time and processing for 20 seconds after each addition, until the dough comes together in large chunks. Transfer the dough to a clean, dry work surface.

3. Alternative method: If you don't have a food processor, combine the flour, sugar, and salt in a large bowl. Add the chilled butter and use a pastry cutter or two knives to cut in the butter until the mixture looks like dry crumbles. Add 2 tablespoons of water and use your hands or a

fork to combine until the dough comes together in large chunks, adding more water as necessary. Transfer the dough to a clean, dry work surface.

4. Gather the dough together and form it into a smooth ball, then press it into a disk. Wrap the disk with plastic wrap.

5. Refrigerate for at least 30 minutes or up to 3 days. After 30 minutes, the dough will be at the perfect temperature and texture to roll. If chilled for longer, let the dough come to room temperature for about 30 minutes before rolling it out. Unless the recipe tells you to fully or partially blind bake the crust, proceed with your pie recipe from this point.

6. **To fully or partially blind bake the crust:** Preheat the oven to 375°F. Lightly spray a pie dish with nonstick baking spray.

7. Roll out the dough on a lightly floured work surface. Fit the dough into the pie dish and crimp as desired. Place a piece of parchment or aluminum foil over the surface of the dough, and let it hang over the sides. Fill the pie dish with dried beans or rice. Freeze the dough for 5 minutes.

8. To fully blind bake the crust, bake for 20 minutes, then remove the pie weights and bake for 15 minutes more. To partially blind bake, bake for 20 minutes, then remove the pie weights, pour in the filling, and continue baking as the recipe indicates.

# Gluten-Free Crust

Makes 1 (9-inch)
single crust
standard pie or
deep-dish pie

Prep time:
10 minutes, plus
30 minutes to chill

Bake time:
20 minutes (par-
tial blind bake) or
35 minutes (full
blind bake)

People who follow a gluten-free diet deserve pie, too! Pie does not discriminate; all are welcome to enjoy. This is an easy piecrust to make, and if you didn't already know it was gluten free, you may not even notice. The crust is made by laminating layers together, emulating a traditional piecrust. This crust can be baked at the same temperatures and same times as the All-Butter Crust, so feel free to use them interchangeably in any recipe.

6 tablespoons (¾ stick; 85 grams) cold unsalted butter

1½ cups (255 grams) 1:1 gluten-free flour blend

1 tablespoon (13 grams) granulated sugar

½ teaspoon salt

¼ teaspoon baking powder

½ cup (123 grams) sour cream

1 to 2 tablespoons ice water

1. Cut the butter into small cubes. Place them in a large metal bowl and put the bowl in the freezer until needed.

2. In a food processor, pulse the flour blend, sugar, salt, and baking powder a few times to combine. Add the butter and process for 30 seconds. Add the sour cream and process until the dough starts to form large crumbles. Add the ice water, 1 tablespoon at a time and processing for 20 seconds after each addition, until the dough comes together in large chunks. Transfer the dough to a clean, dry work surface.

3. Alternative method: If you don't have a food processor, combine the flour blend, sugar, salt, and baking powder in a large bowl. Add the chilled butter and use a pastry cutter or two knives to cut in the butter

until the mixture looks like dry crumbles. Add the sour cream and stir with a wooden spoon until the mixture forms large crumbles. Add the water and use your hands or a fork to combine until the dough comes together in large chunks. Transfer the dough to a clean, dry work surface.

4. Form the dough into a ball. To achieve a flaky crust, roll the dough into an 8-by-8-inch square between two pieces of parchment paper. Fold one half into the center of the dough, then the other half, like folding a letter. Turn the dough 90 degrees and repeat this step twice more. Form the dough into a round disk and wrap with plastic wrap.

5. Chill the dough in the refrigerator for at least 30 minutes or up to 3 days. If chilled for longer than 30 minutes, let it come to room temperature for about 30 minutes before rolling it out. Alternately, freeze the dough for up to 6 months. Unless the recipe tells you to blind or fully bake the crust, proceed with your pie recipe from this point.

6. **To fully or partially blind bake the crust:** Preheat the oven to 375°F. Lightly spray a pie dish with nonstick baking spray.

7. Roll out the dough on a lightly floured work surface. Fit the dough into the pie dish and crimp as desired. Place a piece of parchment or aluminum foil over the surface of the dough, and let it hang over the sides. Fill the pie dish with dried beans or rice. Freeze the dough for 5 minutes.

8. To fully blind bake the crust, bake for 20 minutes, then remove the pie weights and bake for 15 minutes more. To partially blind bake, bake for 20 minutes, then remove the pie weights, pour in the filling, and continue baking as the recipe indicates.

# Whole-Wheat Crust

Makes 1 (9-inch)
single crust
standard pie or
deep-dish pie

Prep time:
10 minutes, plus
30 minutes to chill

Bake time:
20 minutes (par-
tial blind bake) or
35 minutes (full
blind bake)

Whole-wheat flour gives pie dough a sweet, almost nutty flavor that complements nearly any filling.

8 tablespoons (1 stick; 113 grams) cold unsalted butter
¾ cup (90 grams) whole-wheat flour
½ cup (64 grams) all-purpose flour

1½ teaspoons granulated sugar
¼ teaspoon salt
2 to 3 tablespoons ice water

1. Cut the butter into small cubes. Place them in a large metal bowl and put the bowl in the freezer until needed.

2. In a food processor, pulse the whole-wheat flour, all-purpose flour, sugar, and salt to combine. Add the chilled butter cubes and process for 30 seconds or until the mixture looks like dry crumbles. Add the ice water, 1 tablespoon at a time and processing for 20 seconds after each addition, until the dough comes together in large chunks. Transfer the dough to a clean, dry work surface.

3. Alternative method: If you don't have a food processor, combine the whole-wheat and all-purpose flours, sugar, and salt in a large bowl. Add the chilled butter and use a pastry cutter or two knives to cut in the butter until the mixture looks like dry crumbles. Add 2 tablespoons of water and use your hands or a fork to combine until the dough comes together in large chunks, adding more water as necessary. Transfer the dough to a clean, dry work surface.

4. Gather the dough together and form it into a smooth ball, then press it into a disk. Wrap the disk with plastic wrap.

5. Refrigerate for at least 30 minutes or up to 3 days. After 30 minutes, the dough will be at the perfect temperature and texture to roll. If chilled for longer, let it come to room temperature for about 30 minutes before rolling it out. Unless the recipe tells you to blind or fully bake the crust, proceed with your pie recipe from this point.

6. **To fully or partially blind bake the crust:** Preheat the oven to 375°F. Lightly spray a pie dish with nonstick baking spray.

7. Roll out the dough on a lightly floured work surface. Fit the dough into the pie dish and crimp as desired. Place a piece of parchment or aluminum foil over the surface of the dough, and let it hang over the sides. Fill the pie dish with dried beans or rice. Freeze the dough for 5 minutes.

8. To fully blind bake the crust, bake for 20 minutes, then remove the pie weights and bake for 15 minutes more. To partially blind bake, bake for 20 minutes, then remove the pie weights, pour in the filling, and continue baking as the recipe indicates.

# Cornmeal Crust

Makes 1 (9-inch)
single crust
standard pie or
deep-dish pie

Prep time:
10 minutes, plus
30 minutes to chill

Bake time:
20 minutes (par-
tial blind bake) or
35 minutes (full
blind bake)

Cornmeal is a flavor that pairs well with both sweet and savory pies, with a fresh fruit pie or a gooey, cheesy hand pie. This recipe has just a touch of honey to enhance the sweetness of the corn. The finer the cornmeal, the better, but polenta will also work if you can't find cornmeal.

6 tablespoons (¾ stick; 85 grams) cold unsalted butter

1 cup (145 grams) all-purpose flour

½ cup (75 grams) cornmeal

1½ teaspoons granulated sugar

1½ teaspoons honey

¼ teaspoon salt

1 large egg

1 to 2 tablespoons ice water

1. Cut the butter into small cubes. Place them in a large metal bowl and put the bowl in the freezer until needed.

2. In a food processor, pulse the flour, cornmeal, sugar, honey, and salt to combine. Add the chilled butter cubes and egg. Process for 30 seconds or until the mixture looks like dry crumbles. Add the ice water, 1 tablespoon at a time and processing for 20 seconds after each addition, until the dough comes together in large chunks. Transfer the dough to a clean, dry work surface.

3. Alternative method: If you don't have a food processor, combine the flour, cornmeal, sugar, honey, and salt in a large bowl. Add the chilled butter and use a pastry cutter or two knives to cut in the butter until the mixture looks like dry crumbles. Add 2 tablespoons of water and use your hands or a fork to combine until the dough comes together in large chunks, adding more water as necessary. Transfer the dough to a clean, dry work surface.

4. Gather the dough together and form it into a smooth ball, then press it into a disk. Wrap the disk with plastic wrap.

5. Refrigerate the dough for at least 30 minutes or up to 3 days. After 30 minutes, the dough will be at the perfect temperature and texture to roll. If chilled for longer, let it come to room temperature for about 30 minutes before rolling it out. Unless the recipe tells you to blind or fully bake the crust, proceed with your pie recipe from this point.

6. **To fully or partially blind bake the crust:** Preheat the oven to 375°F. Lightly spray a pie dish with nonstick baking spray.

7. Roll out the dough on a lightly floured work surface. Fit the dough into the pie dish and crimp as desired. Place a piece of parchment or aluminum foil over the surface of the dough, and let it hang over the sides. Fill the pie dish with dried beans or rice. Freeze the dough for 5 minutes.

8. To fully blind bake the crust, bake for 20 minutes, then remove the pie weights and bake for 15 minutes more. To partially blind bake, bake for 20 minutes, then remove the pie weights, pour in the filling, and continue baking as the recipe indicates.

# Cocoa Crust

**Makes 1 (9-inch)
single crust
standard pie or
deep-dish pie**

**Prep time:**
10 minutes, plus
30 minutes to chill

**Bake time:**
20 minutes (par-
tial blind bake) or
35 minutes (full
blind bake)

Chocolate makes everything better, right? This cocoa crust is the chocolate version of the All-Butter Crust (page 22). It's sweet but not too sweet, and it adds just a bit more chocolatey richness to pies that already have a little chocolate in them. This crust whips up easily in the food processor and is a simple way to enhance the flavor of your pie.

**8 tablespoons (1 stick; 113 grams) cold unsalted butter**

**1 cup plus 2 tablespoons (162 grams) all-purpose flour**

**2 tablespoons (15 grams) cocoa powder**

**1 tablespoon (13 grams) granulated sugar**

**¼ teaspoon salt**

**2 to 3 tablespoons ice water**

1. Cut the butter into small cubes. Place them in a large metal bowl and put the bowl in the freezer until needed.

2. In a food processor, pulse the flour, cocoa powder, sugar, and salt to combine. Add the chilled butter cubes and process for 30 seconds, or until the mixture looks like dry crumbles. Add the ice water, 1 tablespoon at a time and processing for 20 seconds after each addition, until the dough comes together in large chunks. Transfer the dough to a clean, dry work surface.

3. Alternative method: If you don't have a food processor, combine the flour, cocoa powder, sugar, and salt in a large bowl. Add the chilled butter and use a pastry cutter or two knives to cut in the butter until the mixture looks like dry crumbles. Add 2 tablespoons of water and use

your hands or a fork to combine until the dough comes together in large chunks, adding more water as necessary. Transfer the dough to a clean, dry work surface.

4. Gather the dough together and form it into a smooth ball, then press it into a disk. Wrap the disk with plastic wrap.

5. Refrigerate the dough for at least 30 minutes or up to 3 days. After 30 minutes, the dough will be at the perfect temperature and texture to roll. If chilled for longer, let it come to room temperature for about 30 minutes before rolling it out. Unless the recipe tells you to blind or fully bake the crust, proceed with your pie recipe from this point.

6. **To fully or partially blind bake the crust:** Preheat the oven to 375°F. Lightly spray a pie dish with nonstick baking spray.

7. Roll out the dough on a lightly floured work surface. Fit the dough into the pie dish and crimp as desired. Place a piece of parchment or aluminum foil over the surface of the dough, and let it hang over the sides. Fill the pie dish with dried beans or rice. Freeze the dough for 5 minutes.

8. To fully blind bake the crust, bake for 20 minutes, then remove the pie weights and bake for 15 minutes more. To partially blind bake, bake for 20 minutes, then remove the pie weights, pour in the filling, and continue baking as the recipe indicates.

# Cookie Crust

Cookie crusts are incredibly easy—they are simply crushed cookies mixed with melted butter and usually some sugar—and they are the base of some of the most delicious pies out there. Graham cracker crust is probably the most popular, but you can make a crust with gingersnaps or chocolate sandwich cookies. A hint of salt mixed in the crust cuts the sweetness a bit. It's easiest to count the number of cookies needed for each crust, but sometimes you can find boxes of graham cracker crumbs, so you'll find cup measurements for those in the recipes as well. These recipes give you a nice thick crust on the bottom and sides. Whichever cookie crust flavor you choose, be sure it complements the filling. Also, different recipes will have you make this recipe to different points—either raw or partially or fully baked, so be sure to double-check what the recipe wants you to start with.

Makes 1 (9-inch)
single-crust pie

Prep time:
10 minutes, plus
10 minutes to
chill if making a
no-bake pie

Bake time:
8 minutes

**For a graham cracker crust**

12 graham cracker sheets or 2 cups (168 g) graham cracker crumbs

¼ cup (60 g) granulated sugar

¼ teaspoon salt

8 tablespoons (1 stick; 113 g) unsalted butter, melted, at room temperature

**For a chocolate sandwich cookie crust**

24 chocolate sandwich cookies

¼ teaspoon salt

5 tablespoons (70 g) unsalted butter, melted, at room temperature

continues

**Cookie Crust** continued

**For a gingersnap cookie crust**

40 gingersnap cookies

¼ cup (60 g) granulated sugar

¼ teaspoon salt

6 tablespoons (84 g) unsalted butter, melted, at room temperature

1. Preheat the oven to 350°F (if the pie recipe calls for baking).

2. In a food processor, pulse the cookies, salt, and sugar (if making the graham cracker or ginger-snap crust) to combine. With the motor running, slowly drizzle in the melted butter and process until the mixture appears wet and crumbly. Transfer the contents to a 9-inch pie dish.

3. Alternative method: If you don't have a food processor, very finely crush the cookies in a large, heavy-duty resealable plastic bag using a mallet or rolling pin. Transfer the crumbs to a large bowl and stir in any sugar and salt the recipe calls for as well as the butter, until the mixture looks wet and crumbly. Transfer the contents to a 9-inch pie dish.

4. Using the bottom of a small measuring cup, press the crumbs evenly into the dish, creating a ½-inch border around the edge.

5. Bake for 8 minutes. Let cool to room temperature before filling. If making a no-bake pie, chill the crust in the refrigerator for 10 minutes before filling.

Raspberry-
Peach
Streusel Pie
page 48

# Fruit Pies

# Blueberry Crumble Pie

Makes 1 (9-inch) pie

Prep time:
20 minutes, plus
3 hours to cool

Bake time:
55 minutes

A brown-sugar-cinnamon crumble turns ordinary blueberry pie into something sublime. Just as sublime, it's a very easy pie to make.

**1 All-Butter Crust (page 22) or Gluten-Free Crust (page 24)**

**Flour, for dusting**

**For the filling**

**6 cups blueberries, fresh or frozen, divided**

**1 apple, peeled, cored, and grated**

**2 teaspoons grated lemon zest**

**2 teaspoons freshly squeezed lemon juice**

**¾ cup granulated sugar**

**2 tablespoons cornstarch**

**⅛ teaspoon salt**

**For the crumble topping**

**¾ cup all-purpose flour**

**3 tablespoons packed light brown sugar**

**½ teaspoon ground cinnamon**

**¼ teaspoon salt**

**5 tablespoons unsalted butter, melted and cooled slightly**

1.  **Roll out the crust:** Unwrap the dough onto a lightly floured work surface. Lightly flour a rolling pin and begin rolling the dough from the center outward. Turn the dough 90 degrees and roll again. Continue to turn and roll until you have a roughly 16-inch circle. Roll the dough onto the rolling pin, then unroll it onto a 9-inch pie dish, leaving a 1-inch overhang around the edge. Trim off any excess dough. Fold the overhang underneath around the edge, crimping as you go. Refrigerate while you prepare the filling.

2. **Make the filling:** Place 3 cups of blueberries in a medium saucepan set over medium heat. Mash the berries to release their juices. Cook, stirring frequently, until about half of the berries have broken down and the mixture is thickened and reduced to 1½ cups, about 8 minutes. Let cool.

3. In a large bowl, mix together the cooked berries and the remaining 3 cups of berries along with the apple, lemon zest, lemon juice, sugar, cornstarch, and salt.

4. Position a rack in the lower third of the oven. Preheat the oven to 400°F.

5. **For the crumble topping:** In a medium bowl, combine the flour, sugar, cinnamon, and salt. Pour in the butter. Stir to combine.

6. Pour the filling into the crust. Sprinkle the crumble topping over the top.

7. Place the pie dish on a baking sheet and bake for 20 minutes. Reduce the temperature to 375°F and bake for 30 to 35 minutes more, until the topping has browned and the blueberry filling is bubbling. Cool on a wire rack for 3 hours before serving.

# Roasted Strawberry Slab Pie with Balsamic Drizzle

Slab pie is great for potlucks, and depending on your thoughts on the ideal ratio of crust to filling, perhaps even better than regular pie. It's made in a jelly-roll pan, creating a big batch pie with more crust per slice than a regular pie.

Double batch Cornmeal Crust
 (page 28)
Flour, for dusting
2 pounds fresh or (thawed) frozen
 strawberries
¼ cup cornstarch
¼ cup packed brown sugar

2 tablespoons freshly squeezed
 lemon juice
¼ teaspoon freshly ground
 black pepper
2 tablespoons aged
 balsamic vinegar

Makes 1
(15-by-18-inch)
slab pie

Prep time:
30 minutes, plus
1 hour to cool

Bake time:
35 minutes

1. Unwrap the dough onto a lightly floured work surface. Lightly flour a rolling pin and begin rolling from the center outward. Roll the dough into a 16-by-19-inch rectangle. Drape the dough over the rolling pin, then transfer to a jelly-roll pan. Trim and crimp the edges. Freeze the pan for 10 minutes.

2. Preheat the oven to 400°F.

3. In a large bowl, combine the strawberries, cornstarch, brown sugar, lemon juice, and pepper. Toss until evenly coated. Pour the filling into the jelly-roll pan.

4. Bake for 30 minutes. Turn on the broiler to high and broil for 2 minutes to char the strawberries. Remove from the oven and drizzle the balsamic vinegar over the top. Cool on a wire rack at room temperature for 1 hour before serving.

# Strawberry-Rhubarb Lattice Pie

This pie is the epitome of spring. It's beautifully pink, and the combination of sweet strawberries and sour rhubarb is a match made in heaven. Load it into a flaky, tender all-butter crust, and you'll soon understand why rhubarb is amazing.

4 cups sliced rhubarb (5 or 6 stalks)
3 cups quartered fresh strawberries
½ cup granulated sugar
¼ cup packed light brown sugar
¼ cup cornstarch
¼ teaspoon salt
Zest and juice of 1 lemon
1 large egg

1 tablespoon water
Nonstick baking spray
Double batch All-Butter Crust
 (page 22) or Gluten-Free Crust
 (page 24)
Flour, for dusting
1 teaspoon cold unsalted
 butter, cubed

Makes 1 (9-inch)
double-crust pie

Prep time:
35 minutes, plus
10 minutes to chill
and 1 hour to cool

Bake time:
1 hour 30 minutes

1.  In a large bowl, combine the rhubarb and strawberries.

2.  In a small bowl, mix together the granulated sugar, brown sugar, corn-starch, salt, lemon zest, and lemon juice with a rubber spatula. Fold the mixture into the fruit until thoroughly coated. Set aside.

3.  In a separate small bowl, whisk together the egg and water. Set aside.

4.  Preheat the oven to 350°F. Lightly coat a 9-inch pie dish with baking spray.

5.  Unwrap one dough disk onto a lightly floured work surface. Lightly flour a rolling pin and begin rolling the dough from the center outward. Turn the dough 90 degrees and roll again. Continue to turn and roll until you have a roughly 16-inch circle. Roll the dough onto the rolling pin, then

continues

unroll it onto the pie dish. Press the dough lightly around the edge and into every crevice so the pie dough fills the dish. Let the edge of the dough hang off for now.

6. Fill the pie shell with the strawberry-rhubarb filling, including all the juices from the bowl. Dot the filling with the cold cubed butter.

7. **Prepare the lattice crust:** Unwrap the second dough disk and roll it into a 16-inch circle. Cut 10 (1-inch) strips from it. To weave a lattice top, place 5 dough strips horizontally across the top of the pie, about 1 inch apart. Pull back 3 alternate strips to the center and lay down 1 strip vertically. Replace the horizontal pieces. Pull the other 2 horizontal strips toward the center, stopping at the first vertical strip. Position another vertical strip; replace the 2 horizontal pieces. Repeat with the first 3 horizontal strips to finish one side of the pie. Repeat the process on the other side. Trim the edges of the dough to hang ½ inch over the pie dish edge. Seal and crimp.

8. Using a pastry brush, brush the egg wash over the crust. Place the pie in the refrigerator for 10 minutes.

9. Put a baking sheet on a rack underneath the pie in the oven in case anything bubbles over. Bake for 1 hour 30 minutes until the filling is bubbly and the crust is evenly golden. Cool on a wire rack at room temperature for 1 hour before serving.

10. This pie is best served the day it's made. It can be covered with plastic wrap and refrigerated for up to 3 days or frozen for up to 1 month.

**Tip:** Raspberry and rhubarb is a fantastic flavor combination, too. Raspberries have a deeper, sweeter flavor than strawberries that balances the tartness of the rhubarb. Simply use fresh raspberries in place of the strawberries and prepare the recipe as instructed.

# Summer Peach Galette

Galettes are wonderful because you can change the fruit to whatever you'd like and what's in season. Plus, you don't need a pie dish or tart pan to make it. It's a really simple and delicious dessert that you can make at a moment's notice, but it's still special enough to wow guests.

1 All-Butter Crust (page 22) or
   Gluten-Free Crust (page 24)
Flour, for dusting
5 peaches, cut into ½-inch-
   thick slices
3 tablespoons packed brown sugar
2 tablespoons unsalted butter
1 teaspoon ground cinnamon

½ teaspoon ground ginger
Juice of ½ lemon
Pinch salt
1 large egg, beaten
Coarse turbinado sugar, for topping
Ice cream or whipped cream, for
   serving (optional)

Makes 1
(9-inch) galette

Prep time:
30 minutes

Bake time:
30 minutes

1. Line a baking sheet with parchment paper.

2. Unwrap the dough onto a lightly floured work surface. Lightly flour a rolling pin and begin rolling the dough from the center outward. Turn the dough 90 degrees and roll again. Continue to turn and roll until you have a 10-inch circle, about ⅛ inch thick. Roll the dough onto the rolling pin, then unroll it onto the prepared baking sheet and place it in the refrigerator.

3. In a medium sauté pan over low heat, mix together the peaches, brown sugar, butter, cinnamon, ginger, lemon juice, and salt. Cook until the peaches are slightly tender. Remove from the heat and let cool completely.

4. Preheat the oven to 350°F.

continues

5. Arrange the cooled peaches in the center of the rolled-out dough, leaving about a 2-inch margin around the edges. Fold the dough toward the center and over the filling all the way around, leaving most of the filling showing, pleating the dough as you work. Brush the edges of the dough with the egg and sprinkle with turbinado sugar.

6. Bake for 25 to 30 minutes, or until the edges are nicely browned and the peaches are tender.

7. Serve warm with a scoop of ice cream or a dollop of whipped cream (if using).

**Tip:** When cooking the peaches on the stove, I like to cook them just until they are soft enough to cut with a fork but still have a bit of bite to them. They will continue to cook in the oven, so you're only looking to soften them a bit. If your peaches are very ripe, skip the cooking step and just combine the fruit with the other ingredients in a bowl.

# Raspberry-Peach Streusel Pie

**Makes 1 (9-inch) pie**

**Prep time:**
25 minutes, plus
10 minutes to chill
and 2 hours to cool

**Bake time:**
1 hour 40 minutes

Peaches and raspberries are often in season at the same time, which is great news, because this flavor combination is special. Raspberries have a deep, slightly tart but sweet flavor that is unique in the berry family, and ripe, juicy peaches complement them perfectly. This pie is gorgeous when sliced because both fruits hold up on their own and display their bright orange and bold rosy-pink colors. The streusel topping is spiced with cinnamon, and the oatmeal gives this pie a chewy-crisp texture in every fruity bite.

**For the filling**

1¼ pounds (4) medium peaches, halved, pitted, and sliced
1 cup granulated sugar
¼ cup cornstarch
½ teaspoon vanilla extract

¼ teaspoon salt
1 tablespoon grated lemon zest
1 tablespoon freshly squeezed lemon juice
3 cups fresh raspberries

**For the streusel topping**

¼ cup all-purpose flour
¼ cup rolled oats
¼ cup packed light brown sugar

¼ teaspoon ground cinnamon
8 tablespoons (1 stick) cold unsalted butter, cubed

**For the crust**

Nonstick baking spray
1 All-Butter Crust (page 22) or Gluten-Free Crust (page 24)

Flour, for dusting

1. **Make the filling:** In a large bowl, fold together the peaches, sugar, cornstarch, vanilla, salt, lemon zest, and lemon juice with a rubber spatula. Gently fold in the raspberries to keep them as intact as possible. Set aside.

2. **Make the streusel topping:** In a food processor, combine the flour, oats, brown sugar, and cinnamon and pulse once. Add the butter and continue to pulse until the mixture has large clumps. If you don't have a food processor, combine the flour, oats, brown sugar, and cinnamon in a medium bowl. Add the butter and use your fingertips to combine the ingredients, smashing the butter into smaller pieces, until the mixture has large clumps. Refrigerate until ready to use.

3. Preheat the oven to 350°F. Lightly coat a 9-inch pie dish with baking spray.

4. **Roll out the crust:** Unwrap one dough disk onto a lightly floured work surface. Lightly flour a rolling pin and begin rolling the dough from the center outward. Turn the dough 90 degrees and roll again. Continue to turn and roll until you have a roughly 16-inch circle. Roll the dough onto the rolling pin, then unroll it onto the pie dish. Press the dough lightly around the edge and into every crevice so the pie dough fills the dish. Trim the edge of the dough to hang ½ inch over the edge of the pie dish. Fold the dough under and crimp. Place the dish in the freezer for 10 minutes.

5. Fill the pie shell with the filling, including all the juices from the bowl.

6. Put a baking sheet on a rack underneath the pie in the oven in case anything bubbles over. Bake for 45 minutes. Remove the pie from the oven and sprinkle the chilled topping over the top, leaving some of the raspberry-peach filling exposed. Bake for 55 minutes more. Cool on a wire rack at room temperature for 2 hours before serving.

7. This pie is best served the day it's made. It can be covered with plastic wrap and refrigerated for up to 3 days or frozen for up to 1 month.

**Tip:** Top with some homemade whipped cream, mixing in 1 tablespoon of clear Chambord.

# Fresh Cherry Pie

Makes 1 (9-inch) pie

Prep time:
20 minutes, plus
3 hours to cool

Cook time:
1 hour 5 minutes

This delicious pie is nothing like the cherry pies made with canned filling you've probably had. Splashes of vanilla and almond extract bring nuanced flavors to this summer classic.

**For the crust**

**Double batch All-Butter Crust (page 22) or Gluten-Free Crust (page 24)**

**Flour, for dusting**

**1 large egg**

**1 tablespoon water**

**Coarse turbinado sugar, for topping**

**For the filling**

**5 cups sweet cherries, pitted and halved**

**¾ cup granulated sugar**

**3 tablespoons cornstarch**

**½ teaspoon salt**

**¼ teaspoon almond extract**

**1 teaspoon vanilla extract**

**1 tablespoon freshly squeezed lemon juice**

**2 tablespoons unsalted butter, cut into cubes**

1. **Roll out the crust:** Unwrap one dough disk onto a lightly floured work surface. Lightly flour a rolling pin and begin rolling the dough from the center outward. Turn the dough 90 degrees and roll again. Continue to turn and roll until you have a roughly 16-inch circle. Roll the dough onto the rolling pin, then unroll it onto a 9-inch pie dish, leaving a 1-inch overhang around the edge. Trim off any excess dough. Refrigerate while you make the filling.

2. In a small bowl, beat together the egg and water until well combined. Set aside.

3. Position a rack in the lower third of the oven. Preheat the oven to 425°F.

4. **Make the filling:** In a large bowl, stir together the cherries, sugar, cornstarch, salt, almond extract, vanilla, and lemon juice. Spoon the filling into the crust, leaving some of the liquid in the bowl. Scatter the butter over the filling.

5. **Roll out the top crust:** Unwrap the second disk of pie dough onto a lightly floured work surface. Roll it into a 16-inch circle. Place it over the filling, leaving a 1-inch overhang around the edge. Trim off any excess dough. Working around the edge, fold the top and bottom overhang under, crimping the edge as you go. Cut a few slits in the top crust to allow steam to escape. Lightly brush the crust with the egg wash. Sprinkle turbinado sugar over the top.

6. Place the pie dish on a baking sheet and bake for 15 minutes. Reduce the temperature to 350°F and bake 45 to 50 minutes more, or until the crust is golden brown and the filling is bubbling. Cover the edge of the pie with aluminum foil if they are browning too quickly. Cool on a wire rack at room temperature for 3 hours.

**Tip:** You can also use frozen cherries. Thaw them before using and be sure to drain any excess liquid, as it will seep into the pie dough.

# Purple Sweet Potato Pie Brûlée

Makes 1 (9-inch)
deep-dish pie

Prep time:
1 hour 15 minutes,
plus 2 hours
10 minutes to chill

Bake time:
45 minutes

This pie has a vibrant, dramatic color. Bright purple potatoes make for a wonderful twist on the classic sweet potato pie.

1¼ pounds purple sweet potatoes (2 or 3 potatoes)
1 All-Butter Crust (page 22) or Gluten-Free Crust (page 24)
Flour, for dusting
1 (12-ounce) can evaporated milk
¾ cup granulated sugar, divided
3 large eggs

3 tablespoons unsalted butter, melted
1 teaspoon vanilla extract
½ teaspoon ground cinnamon
½ teaspoon ground ginger
½ teaspoon salt
¼ teaspoon ground nutmeg

1. Prick the sweet potatoes all over with a fork and microwave for about 5 minutes or until tender. Cool completely.

2. Preheat the oven to 350°F.

3. On a lightly floured surface, roll the dough into a 16-inch circle. Transfer the dough to a deep-dish pie dish. Trim and crimp the edge. Freeze for 10 minutes.

4. In a food processor, combine the cooled flesh of the sweet potatoes (discard the skin), evaporated milk, ½ cup of sugar, eggs, butter, vanilla, cinnamon, ginger, salt, and nutmeg. Purée until smooth.

5. Pour the filling into the crust. Bake for 45 minutes. Refrigerate for at least 2 hours.

6. To serve, sprinkle the remaining ¼ cup of sugar over the top of the pie. Use a kitchen torch to caramelize the sugar.

# Ginger and Spice Pumpkin Pie

Fresh ginger along with cinnamon and cloves give a flavorful kick to this classic pie filling. By using canned pumpkin purée, this festive dessert can be pulled together in a matter of minutes. For even quicker prep, you can use a store-bought piecrust. Serve it for Thanksgiving or any special holiday meal with lots of sweetened whipped cream on top.

Makes 1 (9-inch) pie

Prep time:
10 minutes

Cook time:
50 minutes

1 All-Butter Crust (page 22) or
  Gluten-Free Crust (page 24)
1 (15-ounce) can pure pumpkin purée
¾ cup granulated sugar
¾ cup heavy (whipping) cream

2 large eggs
1 tablespoon grated fresh ginger
½ teaspoon ground cinnamon
¼ teaspoon salt
Pinch ground cloves
Whipped cream, for serving

1. Preheat the oven to 350°F.

2. **Roll out the crust:** Unwrap the dough onto a lightly floured work surface. Lightly flour a rolling pin and begin rolling the dough from the center outward. Turn the dough 90 degrees and roll again. Continue to turn and roll until you have a roughly 16-inch circle. Roll the dough onto the rolling pin, then unroll it onto a 9-inch pie dish, leaving a 1-inch overhang around the edge. Trim off any excess dough. Fold the overhang underneath around the edge, crimping as you go. Refrigerate while you prepare the filling.

continues

3.  In a large bowl, whisk the pumpkin purée, sugar, cream, eggs, ginger, cinnamon, salt, and cloves until thoroughly combined. Spoon the mixture into the piecrust, smoothing the top with a rubber spatula.

4.  Bake for 40 to 50 minutes, until the filling is just set in the center. Cool on a wire rack. Serve warm, dolloped with whipped cream.

**Tip:** This pie keeps well in the refrigerator, covered, for up to 2 days. Bring it to room temperature before serving.

# All-American Apple Pie

**Makes 1 (9-inch)
double-crust pie**

**Prep time:**
25 minutes, plus
10 minutes to chill
and 1 hour to cool

**Bake time:**
1 hour 30 minutes

Apple pie, the favorite of—almost—everyone. It's a cure for the blues, a treat for a job well done, or for any occasion, really, just to make people smile. The comforting spices and bright apple flavor always please. The firm texture of Granny Smith apples holds up well in the heat of the oven, and they have a nice tartness. Use whichever variety of apple you like best, keeping in mind that many red varieties have a softer texture and tend to turn to applesauce during the bake. A good way to reheat a slice of apple pie is to broil it in the oven for 2 minutes or heat in a 350°F oven for 5 minutes.

### For the filling

2½ pounds Granny Smith apples, peeled, cored, and sliced (about 6 apples)

½ cup packed light brown sugar

¼ cup granulated sugar

¼ cup cornstarch

½ teaspoon salt

½ teaspoon ground cinnamon

¼ teaspoon ground nutmeg

¼ teaspoon ground allspice

2 tablespoons freshly squeezed lemon juice

1 tablespoon cold unsalted butter, cubed

### For the crust

Nonstick baking spray

Double batch All-Butter Crust (page 22) or Gluten-Free Crust (page 24)

1 large egg

1 tablespoon water

1. **Make the filling:** In a large bowl, mix together the apples, brown sugar, granulated sugar, cornstarch, salt, cinnamon, nutmeg, allspice, and lemon juice, and toss with a rubber spatula until the apples are evenly coated. Set aside.

2. Preheat the oven to 350°F. Lightly coat a 9-inch pie dish with baking spray.

3. **Roll out the crust:** Unwrap one dough disk onto a lightly floured work surface. Lightly flour a rolling pin and begin rolling the dough from the center outward. Turn the dough 90 degrees and roll again. Continue to turn and roll until you have a roughly 16-inch circle. Roll the dough onto your rolling pin, then unroll it onto the pie dish. Press the dough lightly around the edge and into every crevice so the pie dough fills the dish. Let the edge of the dough hang off for now.

4. Add the filling to the pie dish, including all the juices from the bowl. Dot the filling with the cold cubed butter. In a small bowl, whisk together the egg and water. Using a pastry brush, brush the egg wash over the edge of the dough in the pie dish.

5. **Roll out the top crust:** Unwrap the second dough disk and roll it out to a 16-inch circle. Roll the dough onto the rolling pin, then unroll it over the filling. Trim the edge of the dough to hang ½ inch over the edge of the pie dish. Fold the dough under to seal and crimp. Brush the egg wash over the dough. Cut an "X" into the center of the dough and 4 to 6 slits near the edge of the pie for vents. Place the dish in the freezer for 10 minutes.

6. Bake for 1 hour 30 minutes, until the filling is bubbly and the crust is evenly golden. Cool on a wire rack at room temperature for 1 hour before serving.

7. This pie is best served the day it's made. It can be covered with plastic wrap and refrigerated for up to 3 days or frozen for up to 1 month.

**Tip:** Instead of covering the pie with a top crust, use the dough to punch out leaf shapes with cookie cutters and decorate the top of the pie instead. Brush each dough leaf with egg wash and bake as instructed.

# Apple-Cheddar Pie

Makes 1 (9-inch) pie

Prep time:
25 minutes, plus
10 minutes to chill
and 1 hour to cool

Bake time:
1 hour 30 minutes

Apple and Cheddar? Yeah, it's a thing—and it's delicious! Shredded sharp Cheddar cheese is added to the pie dough, which makes it taste like a cheesy cracker but with the same flaky texture of piecrust. After this you may just start experimenting with other sweet-savory options of your own.

**For the crust**

Double batch All-Butter Crust (page 22) or Gluten-Free Crust (page 24)

1½ cups shredded sharp Cheddar cheese

1 large egg

1 tablespoon water

Nonstick baking spray

Flour, for dusting

**For the filling**

2½ pounds Granny Smith apples, peeled, cored, and sliced (about 6 apples)

½ cup packed light brown sugar

¼ cup granulated sugar

¼ cup cornstarch

½ teaspoon ground cinnamon

¼ teaspoon ground nutmeg

¼ teaspoon ground allspice

½ teaspoon salt

2 tablespoons freshly squeezed lemon juice

1 tablespoon cold unsalted butter, cubed

1. **Make the crust:** Make a double batch of All-Butter Crust (page 22) or Gluten-Free Crust (page 24), adding the cheese with the dry ingredients. In a small bowl, whisk together the egg and water. Set aside.

2. **Make the filling:** In a large bowl, mix together the apples, brown sugar, granulated sugar, cornstarch, cinnamon, nutmeg, allspice, salt, and lemon juice with a rubber spatula until thoroughly coated. Set aside.

3. Preheat the oven to 350°F. Lightly coat a 9-inch pie dish with baking spray.

4. **Roll out the crust:** Unwrap one dough disk onto a lightly floured work surface. Lightly flour a rolling pin and begin rolling the dough from the center outward. Turn the dough 90 degrees and roll again. Continue to turn and roll until you have a roughly 16-inch circle. Roll the dough onto the rolling pin, then unroll it onto the prepared pie dish. Press the dough lightly around the edge and into every crevice so the pie dough fills the dish. Let the edge of the dough hang off for now.

5. Fill the pie shell with the apple filling, including all the juices in the bowl. Dot the filling with the cold cubed butter. Using a pastry brush, brush the egg wash over the edges of the dough in the pie dish.

6. **Roll out the top crust:** Unwrap the second dough disk and roll the dough into a 16-inch circle. Roll the dough onto the rolling pin, then unroll it over the filling. Trim the edge of the dough to hang ½ inch over the edge of the pie dish. Fold the dough under to seal and crimp. Brush the egg wash over the dough. Cut an "X" into the center of the dough and 4 to 6 slits near the edge of the pie for vents. Place the dish in the freezer for 10 minutes.

7. Bake for 1 hour 30 minutes, until the filling is bubbly and the crust is evenly golden. Cool on a wire rack at room temperature for 1 hour before serving.

**Tip:** You can easily turn this recipe into hand pies. Halve the measurements of the crust and filling ingredients; omit the butter. Prepare the crust. Cook the filling over medium heat until thickened; cool completely in the refrigerator. Roll the crust to 16 inches and use a 4-inch round cookie cutter to cut 8 to 10 circles. Brush the edges with egg wash and fill each with 2 tablespoons of cooled filling. Fold one side of the dough up and over the filling, making a half-moon shape. Seal and crimp with a fork. Place the hand pies on a parchment-paper-lined baking sheet. Brush the tops with egg wash and poke a few holes to vent. Freeze for 10 minutes; bake in a preheated 425°F oven for 20 minutes, or until bubbly and golden brown.

# Cranberry-Pear Crumble Pie

In this recipe, juicy pears are tossed with cinnamon and tart cranberries, then topped with a crunchy oatmeal streusel, resulting in a pie that might just take center stage at your holiday table.

Makes 1 (9-inch) pie

Prep time:
30 minutes, and
3 hours to cool

Cook time:
55 minutes

### For the crust

1 All-Butter Crust (page 22) or
Gluten-Free Crust (page 24)

Flour, for dusting

### For the filling

5 cups ½-inch diced pears, such as Green Anjou, Bosc, or Bartlett (4 or 5 pears)

1¾ cups cranberries, fresh or frozen

1 tablespoon freshly squeezed lemon juice

⅓ cup all-purpose flour

½ cup granulated sugar

1½ teaspoons ground cinnamon

### For the topping

1 cup all-purpose flour

¾ cup light brown sugar

⅓ cup granulated sugar

½ teaspoon ground cinnamon

¼ teaspoon salt

8 tablespoons (1 stick) unsalted butter, melted

½ cup old-fashioned oats

1. **Roll out the dough:** Unwrap the dough onto a lightly floured work surface. Lightly flour a rolling pin and begin rolling the dough from the center outward. Turn the dough 90 degrees and roll again. Continue to turn and roll until you have a roughly 16-inch circle. Roll the dough onto the rolling pin, then unroll it onto a 9-inch pie dish, leaving a 1-inch overhang around the edge. Trim off any excess dough. Fold the overhang underneath around the edge, crimping as you go. Refrigerate while you prepare the filling.

continues

## Cranberry-Pear Crumble Pie continued

2. **Make the filling:** In a large bowl, gently mix together all the filling ingredients until combined. Spoon the filling into the crust. Refrigerate the pie while making the topping.

3. Position a rack in the lower third of the oven. Preheat the oven to 400°F.

4. **Make the topping:** In a medium bowl, combine the flour, brown sugar, granulated sugar, cinnamon, and salt. Add the butter and mix until the topping has a crumbly texture. Stir in the oats. Sprinkle the topping over the filling.

5. Place the pie dish on a baking sheet and bake for 20 minutes. Reduce the temperature to 375°F and bake for 30 to 35 minutes more, until crust is golden and the filling is bubbly. Cool on a wire rack at room temperature for 3 hours.

Maple,
Walnut, and
Bourbon Pie
page 66

# Creamy, Nutty, and Chocolatey Pies

# Maple, Walnut, and Bourbon Pie

Makes 1 (9-inch) pie

Prep time:
15 minutes, plus
10 minutes to chill
and 1 hour to cool

Bake time:
50 minutes

Maple. Walnuts. Bourbon. Do you really need anything else? This is essentially a candied walnut pie with a texture similar to pecan pie. Topped with a boozy bourbon-vanilla whipped cream and dusted with a sprinkling of cinnamon, this is a really nice treat, so go ahead—you only live once.

### For the filling

3 large eggs

1 cup maple syrup

½ cup packed light brown sugar

1½ tablespoons all-purpose flour

2 tablespoons bourbon

1 teaspoon vanilla extract

¼ teaspoon ground cinnamon

2 tablespoons unsalted
   butter, melted

2 cups walnuts

### For the crust

Nonstick baking spray

1 All-Butter Crust (page 22) or
   Gluten-Free Crust (page 24)

Flour, for dusting

### For the whipped cream

1 cup heavy (whipping) cream

½ cup powdered sugar

1 tablespoon bourbon

½ teaspoon vanilla extract

1. **Make the filling:** In a large bowl, whisk together the eggs, maple syrup, and brown sugar. Add the flour, bourbon, vanilla, cinnamon, and butter and whisk to thoroughly combine. Set aside.

2. Preheat the oven to 350°F. Lightly coat a 9-inch pie dish with baking spray.

3. **Roll out the crust:** Unwrap the dough disk onto a lightly floured work surface. Lightly flour a rolling pin and begin rolling the dough from the center outward. Turn the dough 90 degrees and roll again. Continue to turn and roll until you have a roughly 16-inch circle. Roll the dough onto the rolling pin, then unroll it onto the pie dish. Press the dough lightly around the edge and into every crevice so the pie dough fills the dish. Trim and crimp the edge. Place the dish in the freezer for 10 minutes.

4. Evenly arrange the walnuts in the pie shell. Pour the filling over the walnuts and smooth it out with a rubber spatula, making sure the walnuts are evenly distributed.

5. Bake for 45 to 50 minutes, until the center is set and not jiggly. Cool on a wire rack at room temperature for 1 hour before serving.

6. **Make the whipped cream:** In the bowl of a stand mixer fitted with the whisk attachment, or in a large bowl and using a hand mixer, whip the heavy cream, powdered sugar, bourbon, and vanilla until stiff peaks form. Dollop pie slices with whipped cream before serving.

7. This pie is best served the day it's made. It can be stored, uncovered, in the refrigerator for up to 3 days or wrapped with plastic and frozen for up to 1 month.

**Tip:** Swap rum for the bourbon in both the filling and whipped cream.

# Dark Chocolate Pecan Pie

The classic Southern pecan pie gets even better when you add dark chocolate and a splash of bourbon to the filling. Feel free to use a store-bought crust to make this easy pie even easier.

Makes 1 (9-inch) pie

Prep time:
20 minutes, plus
2 hours to cool

Cook time:
40 minutes

1½ cups pecan halves

6 tablespoons (¾ stick) unsalted butter

2 ounces bittersweet chocolate, chopped

¾ cup dark corn syrup

4 large eggs

½ cup packed light brown sugar

1 tablespoon unsweetened cocoa powder

2 tablespoons bourbon

¼ teaspoon salt

1 All-Butter Crust (page 22), 1 Gluten-Free Crust (page 24), or 1 Cocoa Crust (page 30), fitted into a 9-inch pie dish and partially blind baked

1. Preheat the oven to 350°F.

2. Spread the pecans in a single layer on a large rimmed baking sheet. Bake for 8 to 10 minutes, until fragrant and lightly browned. Remove from the oven and let cool. Leave the oven on.

3. While the nuts cool, in a small saucepan over low heat, combine the butter and chocolate. Cook, stirring constantly, until both are melted and the mixture is smooth. Transfer the mixture to a large bowl. Let cool.

4. Add the corn syrup, eggs, brown sugar, cocoa powder, bourbon, and salt to the cooled chocolate mixture and whisk well to combine. Pour the filling into the crust and arrange the pecans in a single layer on top of the filling. Bake for 30 to 40 minutes, until the filling is just barely set.

5. Cool on a wire rack at room temperature for at least 2 hours before serving.

# Black Bottom Peanut Butter Mousse Pie

**Makes 1 (9-inch) pie**

**Prep time:**
40 minutes, plus
4 to 6 hours to chill

This rich and delicious pie conceals a layer of chocolate beneath a creamy peanut butter mousse filling.

**For the fudge layer and crust**

½ cup semisweet chocolate chips

¼ cup heavy (whipping) cream

1 tablespoon unsalted butter, at room temperature

¼ teaspoon vanilla extract

1 unbaked Cookie Crust (page 33), made with chocolate sandwich cookies, pressed into a 9-inch pie dish, refrigerated for 30 minutes

**For the mousse filling**

1 cup cream cheese, at room temperature

⅔ cup powdered sugar

¾ cup smooth peanut butter

1 teaspoon vanilla extract

¾ cup cold heavy (whipping) cream

1. **Make the fudge layer:** In a microwave-safe bowl, combine all the ingredients for the fudge layer. Microwave in 30-second increments, stirring between each increment, until the chocolate is melted and smooth. Pour the mixture into the crust. Freeze for 10 minutes until firm.

2. **Make the mousse filling:** In a medium bowl, using an electric mixer set on medium, mix together the cream cheese and sugar until light and fluffy. Mix in the peanut butter and vanilla.

3. In a separate medium bowl, using an electric mixer, whip the cold cream until soft peaks form, 2 to 3 minutes. Gently fold the whipped cream into the peanut butter mixture. Spread this over the fudge layer. Cover and refrigerate for 4 to 6 hours.

# PB&J Pie

The addition of cream cheese makes this pie taste almost like a peanut butter cheesecake, but the sweet-tartness of the raspberry jam brings you right back to being a kid. Top the pie with a few fresh raspberries for a classy touch.

Makes 1 (9-inch) pie

Prep time:
35 minutes, plus
1 hour 30 minutes
to chill

Bake time:
40 minutes

### For the crust

**Nonstick baking spray**

**1 All-Butter Crust (page 22),**
   **1 Gluten-Free Crust (page 24), or**
   **1 Cocoa Crust (page 30)**

**Flour, for dusting**

### For the peanut butter filling

**1 cup cream cheese, at room temperature**

**1 cup smooth peanut butter**

**½ cup granulated sugar**

**½ teaspoon vanilla extract**

**½ teaspoon salt**

### For the raspberry jam

**3 cups fresh raspberries**

**Juice of 1 lemon**

**½ cup granulated sugar**

**1 teaspoon pectin**

### For the whipped cream

**1 cup cold heavy (whipping) cream**

**½ cup powdered sugar**

**½ teaspoon vanilla extract**

1. Preheat the oven to 375°F. Lightly coat a 9-inch pie dish with baking spray.

2. **Roll out the crust:** Unwrap the dough onto a lightly floured work surface. Lightly flour a rolling pin and begin rolling the dough from the center outward. Turn the dough 90 degrees and roll again. Continue to

continues

turn and roll until you have a roughly 16-inch circle. Roll the dough onto the rolling pin, then unroll it onto the pie dish. Press the dough lightly around the edge and into every crevice so the pie dough fills the dish. Trim the edge of the dough to hang ½ inch over the edge of the pie dish. Fold the dough under and crimp. Place the dish in the freezer for 10 minutes.

3. **Fully blind bake the crust:** Place a sheet of parchment paper or aluminum foil over the dough in the dish, letting the edges hang over. Pour in dried beans or rice and spread them evenly in the dish to help keep the crust flat while it bakes. Bake for 20 minutes, then carefully remove the pie weights and bake for 15 to 20 minutes more. If the crust is evenly golden brown, it is done. Let the crust cool at room temperature.

4. **Make the peanut butter filling:** In the bowl of a stand mixer fitted with a paddle attachment, or in a large bowl and using a hand mixer, mix together the cream cheese and peanut butter until smooth, scraping down the sides of the bowl as needed. Add the sugar, vanilla, and salt and mix until smooth, scraping down the sides as needed. Transfer the filling to the pie shell and smooth it out. Place in the freezer for 20 minutes.

5. **Make the raspberry jam:** In a blender, purée the raspberries until smooth. Strain the purée through a fine-mesh strainer set over a small saucepan, pressing through as much of the purée as possible. Stir in the lemon juice. In a small bowl, whisk together the sugar and pectin and add it to the saucepan. Place the pan over medium-high heat and cook for about 15 minutes, until the purée has reduced and thickened. Pour the raspberry jam over the peanut butter filling, spreading it evenly. Place in the refrigerator for 1 hour to let the raspberry jam set.

6. **Make the whipped cream:** In the bowl of a stand mixer fitted with the whisk attachment, or in a large bowl and using a hand mixer, whip the heavy cream, powdered sugar, and vanilla until stiff peaks form. Spread the whipped cream over the surface of the pie.

**Tip:** Pectin is a compound that helps jam and jelly get their signature soft-but-spoonable texture. It's found naturally in many fruits, but you can buy powdered pectin in the grocery store.

# No-Bake French Silk Pie with Shortbread Crust

Makes 1 (9-inch) pie

Prep time:
20 minutes, plus
3 hours to chill

You won't believe how easy it is to make this rich, creamy chocolate cream pie. The shortbread cookie crumb crust doesn't even need to be baked, and it adds a buttery, crumbly, sweet base layer that may be even better than a regular piecrust. Make this for any special occasion. Like, you know, an average Tuesday night dinner.

**For the crust**

2¾ cups (about 11 ounces) crushed shortbread cookie crumbs

1 tablespoon granulated sugar

6 tablespoons (¾ stick) unsalted butter, melted

**For the filling**

⅔ cup granulated sugar

2 large eggs

2 ounces unsweetened baking chocolate, chopped

⅓ cup unsalted butter, left at room temperature for 15 to 20 minutes before using

1½ cups heavy (whipping) cream

¼ cup powdered sugar

Chocolate shavings, for garnish

1.  **Make the crust:** In a large bowl, stir together the cookie crumbs, sugar, and butter until well combined. Press the mixture into the bottom and up the sides of a 9-inch pie dish. Refrigerate for 1 hour before proceeding with the recipe.

2. **Make the filling:** In a small saucepan, whisk the sugar and eggs until well mixed. Place the pan over medium heat and cook for about 4 minutes, until the mixture is thick enough to coat the back of a spoon. Remove the pan from the heat and stir in the chocolate, stirring until melted and the mixture is smooth. Let cool for a few minutes.

3. Mix in the butter, stirring until it is fully incorporated. Transfer to a large bowl and refrigerate while you make the whipped cream.

4. In another large bowl, use a handheld electric mixer or a stand mixer to whip the cream until it holds soft peaks. Add the powdered sugar and continue to whip until it holds stiff peaks.

5. Add half the whipped cream to the cooled chocolate mixture and gently fold it in with a rubber spatula. Pour the filling into the prepared crust.

6. Dollop the remaining whipped cream on top and garnish with chocolate shavings. Refrigerate for at least 2 hours before serving.

**Tip:** The eggs in this recipe aren't fully cooked. If you are concerned about eating raw or under-cooked eggs, use pasteurized eggs.

# No-Bake Mocha Mud Pie

Makes 1 (9-inch) pie

Prep time:
20 minutes, plus
4 hours to chill

This mud pie strays from the traditional pudding-filled concoction you may be used to, but it fulfills any chocoholic's fantasy, and then some. It's a chocolate cookie crumb crust filled with a rich, espresso-flavored, chocolatey cream cheese mixture, all topped with sweetened whipped cream, chocolate shavings, and hot fudge sauce.

1 tablespoon instant espresso powder

¼ cup water

3 ounces semisweet chocolate, chopped

2 cups heavy (whipping) cream

¾ cup powdered sugar, divided

½ teaspoon vanilla extract

1 (8-ounce) package cream cheese, at room temperature

1 unbaked Cookie Crust (page 33), made with chocolate sandwich cookies, pressed into a 9-inch pie dish, refrigerated for 30 minutes

Chocolate shavings, for garnish

1 cup hot fudge sauce

1. In a measuring cup, mix the espresso powder into the water. Set aside to let the espresso powder dissolve.

2. Meanwhile, in a small microwave-safe bowl, microwave the chocolate at 50 percent power, in 30-second increments, stirring between increments, until melted and smooth.

3. In a large bowl with a handheld electric mixer or in a stand mixer, whip the heavy cream until it holds soft peaks. Add ½ cup of powdered sugar and the vanilla. Whip until the mixture holds stiff peaks.

4. In another large bowl, beat together the cream cheese and remaining ¼ cup of powdered sugar until thoroughly combined. Add the espresso and stir to incorporate completely. Add the melted chocolate and mix to combine.

5. Gently fold 2 cups of whipped cream into the cream-cheese-chocolate mixture. Transfer to the prepared crust and smooth the top with a rubber spatula.

6. Spread the remaining whipped cream on top and garnish with chocolate shavings. Refrigerate the pie for at least 4 hours before serving. Serve with hot fudge sauce drizzled over the top.

**Tip:** This pie is even better the day after it's made, so go ahead and make it in advance. Keep it covered in the refrigerator until ready to serve.

# Salted Honey Pie

It's funny how much a little salt can do for a sweet dessert. In this case, without the salt, the pie would be too sweet, but with it, you can rationalize that extra bite (or two).

Makes 1 (9-inch) pie

Prep time:
20 minutes, plus
10 minutes to chill
and 1 hour to cool

Bake time:
50 minutes

### For the filling

8 tablespoons (1 stick) unsalted butter, melted

¾ cup honey

½ cup sour cream

¼ cup packed light brown sugar

1 tablespoon apple cider vinegar

2 teaspoons cornstarch

1 teaspoon salt

1 teaspoon vanilla extract

3 large eggs

### For the crust

Nonstick baking spray

1 All-Butter Crust (page 22) or Gluten-Free Crust (page 24)

Flour, for dusting

1 teaspoon flaky sea salt, such as Maldon or fleur de sel

1. **Make the filling:** In a food processor, combine all the ingredients for the filling and process until smooth. Set aside.

2. Preheat the oven to 350°F. Lightly coat a 9-inch pie dish with baking spray.

3. **Roll out the crust:** Unwrap the dough onto a lightly floured work surface. Lightly flour a rolling pin and begin rolling the dough from the center outward. Turn the dough 90 degrees and roll again. Continue to turn and roll until you have a roughly 16-inch circle. Roll the dough onto the rolling pin, then unroll it onto the prepared pie dish. Press the dough lightly around the edge and into every crevice so the pie dough fills the dish. Trim and crimp the edge. Place the dish in the freezer for 10 minutes.

continues

4. Pour the honey filling into the pie shell. Bake for 45 to 50 minutes until the filling is set and not jiggly. Cool on a wire rack at room temperature for 1 hour before serving. Sprinkle the sea salt over the top and serve.

5. This pie is best served the day it's made. It can be covered with plastic wrap and refrigerated for up to 3 days or frozen for up to 1 month.

**Tip:** Add 1 tablespoon of minced fresh thyme leaves to the filling ingredients to level up the flavor profile, and follow the recipe as instructed.

# No-Bake Maple Syrup Cream Pie

Maple syrup has one of the most heavenly flavors, and it's not just for covering pancakes and French toast. This delicious no-bake pie delivers intense maple flavor in a creamy, smooth filling. It's a Canadian version of sugar cream pie and is traditionally made to celebrate the springtime syrup-making season.

Makes 1 (9-inch) pie

Prep time:
10 minutes, plus
4 hours to chill

1½ cups maple syrup (see tip)
1 cup heavy (whipping) cream
¼ cup cornstarch mixed with ¼ cup cold water

1 (9-inch) piecrust (prebaked, homemade, or store-bought and baked according to the package directions)

1. In a medium saucepan set over medium-high heat, whisk together the maple syrup and cream. Bring to a simmer. Whisking constantly, add the cornstarch mixture.

2. Still whisking constantly, bring the mixture to a boil and cook for about 2 minutes, lowering the heat if necessary to keep it from burning, until the mixture thickens. Pour the maple-cream mixture into the piecrust and refrigerate for at least 4 hours until set. Serve chilled.

**Tip:** When choosing maple syrup, remember that the darker the color, the more intense the maple flavor will be. Because maple syrup is the star of this show, I like to use a dark amber, or grade B, syrup for this pie.

# Coconut Custard Pie

Makes 1 (9-inch) pie

Prep time:
35 minutes, plus
4 hours 35 minutes
to chill

Bake time:
1 hour 20 minutes

This pie bakes into two distinct layers—crust and custardy filling. You get the creamy, delicious coconut flavor of a coconut cream pie, but with far less effort.

6 tablespoons (¾ stick) unsalted butter, at room temperature, plus more for the pie dish

½ cup all-purpose flour, plus more for the pie dish

1 All-Butter Crust (page 22) or Gluten-Free Crust (page 24)

1 (14-ounce) can sweetened condensed milk

1 (13½-ounce) can coconut milk

4 large eggs

1½ cups sweetened flaked coconut, divided

1 teaspoon vanilla extract

¼ teaspoon salt

1. Grease a 9-inch pie dish with butter and dust it with flour.

2. **Roll out the dough:** Unwrap the disk of pie dough onto a lightly floured work surface. Lightly flour a rolling pin and begin rolling the dough from the center outward. Turn the dough 90 degrees and roll again. Continue to turn and roll until you have a roughly 16-inch circle. Roll the dough onto the rolling pin, then unroll it onto the prepared pie dish. Press the dough lightly around the edge and into every crevice so the pie dough fills the dish. Trim the edge of the dough to hang ½ inch over the edge of the pie dish. Fold the overhang underneath itself around the edge, crimping as you go. Refrigerate for 30 minutes.

3. Preheat the oven to 375°F.

4. Line the dough with parchment paper or aluminum foil. Fill with dried beans or rice. Freeze for 5 minutes, then bake for 20 minutes or until the edge begins to brown. Remove and let cool. Reduce the oven temperature to 350°F.

5. **Make the filling:** In a large bowl, using an electric mixer or a whisk, or in a blender, combine the sweetened condensed milk, coconut milk, eggs, 1 cup of coconut, butter, flour, vanilla, and salt. Beat until smooth. Pour the mixture into the crust.

6. Bake for 50 minutes to 1 hour until the center is mostly set. Cool on a wire rack to room temperature, about 1 hour. Transfer to the refrigerator and chill for at least 4 hours until completely set.

7. Just before serving, sprinkle the remaining ½ cup of coconut over the top. Cut into wedges and serve chilled.

**Tip:** Toasting the coconut makes its flavor deeper and more complex. It looks pretty on top of the pie, too. Spread it on a baking sheet and toast in a 325°F oven for about 5 minutes, stirring occasionally, until golden brown.

# Banana Cream Pie

Makes 1 (9-inch) pie

Prep time:
45 minutes, plus
10 minutes to cool
and 1 hour to chill

Bake time:
10 minutes

Traditionally, the creamy vanilla custard and fresh bananas in this pie are set in a regular piecrust. This recipe uses a quick and easy cookie crust.

**For the crust**

**1 unbaked Cookie Crust (page 33), made with graham cracker crumbs, pressed into a 9-inch pie dish**

**For the filling**

**4 large egg yolks**

**¾ cup granulated sugar**

**⅓ cup cornstarch**

**¼ teaspoon salt**

**2 cups whole milk**

**2 tablespoons unsalted butter, at room temperature**

**1¼ teaspoons vanilla extract**

**2 or 3 bananas, peeled and sliced**

**For the whipped cream**

**1 cup cold heavy (whipping) cream**

**3 tablespoons powdered sugar**

**1 teaspoon vanilla extract**

1. Preheat the oven to 350°F.

2. Bake the crust for 10 minutes. Cool completely before filling.

3. **Make the filling:** In a small bowl, beat the egg yolks and set aside. In a medium saucepan, combine the sugar, cornstarch, and salt. Add the milk gradually while stirring gently. Cook over medium heat, stirring constantly, until the mixture comes to a boil, about 10 minutes. Continue to whisk and cook for about 2 more minutes. Remove from the heat.

4. Stir a small quantity of the hot mixture into the beaten egg yolks, then immediately add the egg yolk mixture to the rest of the hot filling. Return the pan to the heat and cook, whisking constantly, for about 2 minutes. Remove the pan from the heat, then add the butter and vanilla. Stir until the butter is melted and the filling is smooth.

5. Arrange the bananas on the bottom of the piecrust. Pour the custard over the bananas. Allow to cool for 10 minutes, then cover the pie with plastic wrap to prevent a skin from forming on the custard. Refrigerate for 1 hour.

6. **Make the whipped cream:** Using an electric mixer fitted with a whisk attachment and set on medium-high speed, beat the cream, powdered sugar, and vanilla until stiff peaks form, about 5 minutes. Spread onto the chilled pie before serving.

**Tip:** The technique of adding a small amount of hot liquid to the yolks and then stirring the mixture back into the rest of the hot mixture is called tempering. This slowly raises the temperature of the eggs so they don't curdle and you get a smooth filling.

# Key Lime Pie

The first time I tasted key lime pie, I was in heaven. I was shocked to learn that the recipe came from the back of a condensed milk can. This superbly simple version comes together in minutes.

Makes 1 (9-inch) pie

Prep time:
10 minutes, plus
1 hour to chill

Bake time:
20 minutes

1 unbaked Cookie Crust (page 33), made with graham cracker crumbs, pressed into a 9-inch pie dish

2 (14-ounce) cans sweetened condensed milk

¾ cup freshly squeezed key lime juice

½ cup full-fat sour cream

2 teaspoons grated lime zest

1. Position a rack in the middle of the oven. Preheat the oven to 350°F.

2. Bake the crust for 8 minutes or until set and golden. Set aside to cool. Leave the oven on.

3. In a medium bowl, combine the condensed milk, key lime juice, sour cream, and lime zest. Pour the filling into the graham cracker crust.

4. Bake for 8 to 10 minutes or until the filling is set.

5. Refrigerate the pie for at least 1 hour and up to 3 days before serving.

**Tip:** Fresh key limes can be difficult to find, so feel free to use bottled key lime juice.

# Lemon Meringue Pie

Makes 1 (9-inch) pie

Prep time:
1 hour, plus 5 hours
30 minutes to chill

Bake time:
40 minutes

This classic dessert, a combination of pillowy meringue and tart custard, is a labor of love, but the payoff is absolutely worth it.

Nonstick baking spray
1 All-Butter Crust (page 22) or
   Gluten-Free Crust (page 24)

Flour, for dusting

**For the lemon filling**

4 large egg yolks, at room
   temperature
1 cup granulated sugar
6 tablespoons cornstarch
¼ teaspoon salt

1½ cups water
½ cup freshly squeezed lemon juice
1 tablespoon grated lemon zest
2 tablespoons unsalted butter, at
   room temperature

**For the meringue**

4 large egg whites, at room
   temperature

¼ teaspoon cream of tartar
6 tablespoons granulated sugar

1.   Lightly grease a 9-inch pie dish with nonstick spray.

2.   **Roll out the dough:** Unwrap the disk of pie dough onto a lightly floured work surface. Lightly flour a rolling pin and begin rolling the dough from the center outward. Turn the dough 90 degrees and roll again. Continue to turn and roll until you have a roughly 16-inch circle. Roll the dough onto the rolling pin, then unroll it onto the prepared pie dish. Press the dough lightly around the edge and into every crevice so the pie dough fills the dish. Trim the edge of the dough to hang ½ inch over the edge of the pie dish. Fold the overhang underneath itself around the edge, crimping as you go. Refrigerate for 30 minutes.

3. Preheat the oven to 400°F.

4. Line the dough with parchment paper or aluminum foil. Fill with pie weights or dried beans. Bake for about 15 minutes, or until the edge begins to brown. Remove the parchment and weights. Prick the crust all over with a fork. Bake for about 7 minutes more, or until the bottom crust is golden brown. Let cool on a wire rack while you make the filling. Reduce the oven temperature to 350°F.

5. **Make the filling:** In a small bowl, beat the egg yolks and set aside.

6. In a medium saucepan, whisk together the sugar, cornstarch, salt, water, lemon juice, and lemon zest. Cook over medium heat, stirring constantly, until the mixture comes to a boil and visibly thickens, about 10 minutes. Continue to cook while whisking for 2 minutes more. Remove from the heat.

7. Stir a small quantity of the hot lemon mixture into the egg yolks, then immediately stir the egg yolk mixture into the rest of the hot lemon filling. Return the pan to the heat and cook, whisking constantly, for about 2 minutes. Remove the pan from the heat, then add the butter and stir until it is melted and the consistency is smooth. Pour the filling into the cooled piecrust.

8. **Make the meringue:** In a large, dry bowl, use an electric mixer fitted with a whisk attachment set on high to whip the egg whites and cream of tartar together until soft peaks form, about 5 minutes. Add the sugar all at once. Continue beating on high speed until glossy stiff peaks form, about 2 more minutes. Spread the meringue on top of the warm filling, making sure it touches the crust.

9. Bake for 10 to 15 minutes or until the meringue begins to brown. Let cool for 1 hour. Transfer the pie to the refrigerator and chill for 4 hours before slicing and serving. Lemon meringue pie is best enjoyed on the day it is made.

**Tip:** Be sure there is no trace of egg yolk in the whites, which would keep them from whipping properly.

Chicken
Pot Pie
page 102

# 5

# Savory Pies

# Beer Cheese Hand Pies

If you've ever had beer cheese, you know just how irresistibly delicious it is. There is something about beer and cheese that makes you want to keep going back in for another bite. A lightly hopped wheat ale is a great choice for this recipe, but feel free to use your favorite type. Malted and hoppy beers are both great options.

Makes 10 hand pies

Prep time:
35 minutes, plus
1 hour 10 minutes
to chill and
5 minutes to cool

Bake time:
20 minutes

4 tablespoons (½ stick) unsalted butter

¼ cup all-purpose flour

½ teaspoon garlic powder

½ teaspoon onion powder

⅛ teaspoon ground cayenne pepper

½ cup milk

½ cup beer

1 teaspoon stone-ground mustard

½ cup shredded sharp Cheddar cheese

½ cup shredded mozzarella cheese

¼ teaspoon salt

⅛ teaspoon freshly ground black pepper

1 large egg

2 tablespoons water

1 All-Butter Crust (page 22) or Gluten-Free Crust (page 24)

1. In a small saucepan over medium-high heat, melt the butter. Once melted, stir in the flour, garlic powder, onion powder, and cayenne. Add a little milk and stir to combine. Continue to add the milk slowly, then add the beer and mix well. Add the mustard, then fold in the Cheddar and mozzarella and continue to heat until completely melted. Add the salt and pepper and stir. Transfer the beer cheese to a medium bowl, cover the surface of the cheese with plastic wrap, and chill in the refrigerator for 1 hour or until completely cooled.

continues

2. Preheat the oven to 425°F. In a small bowl, whisk together the egg and water. Set aside.

3. Unwrap the dough onto a lightly floured work surface. Lightly flour a rolling pin and begin rolling out the dough from the center outward until it is ⅛ inch thick. Use a 4-inch round cookie cutter to cut out as many circles as possible. Gather any dough scraps together and reroll to the same thickness to cut out more pieces. You should have 10.

4. Line a baking sheet with parchment paper. Brush each circle of dough with egg wash. Place 1 tablespoon of beer cheese inside the center of a dough circle, leaving a ½-inch border around the perimeter. Bring the edges of the dough together, creating a half moon shape. Using a fork, seal the dough around the edges. Place the pie on the prepared baking sheet. Repeat with the remaining beer cheese and dough circles, setting them on the baking sheet about 1 inch apart. Brush the top of each pie with egg wash. Chill in the freezer for 10 minutes.

5. Before baking, use a knife to poke 2 holes on top of each hand pie to vent. Bake for 18 minutes or until the pies are evenly golden brown. Cool on a wire rack at room temperature for 5 minutes and serve immediately.

**Tip:** Did someone say jalapeño beer cheese? Try sprucing up your pies with jalapeño. Just chop up 1 jalapeño and add it to the beer cheese when folding in the cheeses.

# Fig, Gorgonzola, and Pear Tartlets

Fig jam is a staple of cheese plates, but that's not all it's good for. In these flaky tarts, it complements the pears. The sharp Gorgonzola cheese provides a savory note. These tartlets can be made ahead. To reheat before serving, place the tartlets on a parchment-paper-lined baking sheet and bake for 10 minutes at 350°F just before serving.

**Serves 8**

**Prep time:**
15 minutes

**Bake time:**
25 minutes

**1 sheet frozen puff pastry, thawed**

**1 ripe pear, cored and diced**

**¼ cup fig jam**

**⅓ cup Gorgonzola cheese**

1. Preheat the oven to 400°F.

2. Spread the puff pastry on a cutting board or clean work surface. Using a 3-inch cookie or biscuit cutter, or similar-size object, cut the dough into 12 rounds. Press the dough rounds into the cups of a standard-size muffin tin. You may need to gather and reroll the dough to get all 12 rounds.

3. Divide the pear evenly among the dough rounds. Top each with 1 teaspoon of fig jam and a sprinkle of Gorgonzola cheese.

4. Bake for 20 to 25 minutes, or until golden.

5. Gently use a knife around the sides of the tin to release the tarts. Transfer to a serving plate. Enjoy hot or at room temperature.

**Tip:** If desired, sprinkle the tarts with a little extra Gorgonzola cheese before serving. It will increase their savoriness.

# Asparagus, Spinach, and Parmesan Galette with Sunny-Side-Up Eggs

Raise your hand if you're always up for brunch. Sundays are for brunching with friends, and this galette makes the perfect addition to your spread. It's easy and fast to whip up, and you can do a lot of the work ahead of time. Make the dough and cook the asparagus and spinach the day before, then store in your refrigerator. When you're ready for brunch, just construct the galette and bake.

Makes 1
(12-inch) galette

Prep time:
30 minutes, plus
20 minutes to chill

Bake time:
25 minutes

1 (10-ounce) bag fresh spinach

1 teaspoon salt, divided

1 tablespoon olive oil

3 cups chopped asparagus (from 1 bunch)

1 teaspoon minced garlic

1 Whole-Wheat Crust (page 26)

½ cup shredded parmesan cheese

2 large eggs, divided

2 tablespoons water

1. In a large saucepan over medium-high heat, cook the spinach with ½ teaspoon of salt. Toss until fully cooked, then transfer to a medium bowl and chill in the refrigerator. Once cooled, wring out any excess water by pressing the spinach against a fine-mesh strainer. Set aside.

2. In a large skillet over medium-high heat, heat the olive oil. Once hot, add the asparagus, garlic, and remaining ½ teaspoon of salt and cook for 5 minutes or until the asparagus is tender. Transfer to a medium bowl and set aside.

3. Unwrap the dough onto a lightly floured work surface. Lightly flour a rolling pin and begin rolling out the dough from the center outward. Turn the dough 90 degrees and roll again. Continue to turn and roll until you have a roughly 16-inch circle. Drape the dough over the rolling pin, then transfer to a parchment-paper-lined baking sheet.

continues

4. Fill the center of the dough circle with the spinach and asparagus, leaving a clear 2-inch border. Top with the parmesan cheese. Fold the edges of the dough in, on top of the filling. Use a spoon to make an indentation in the center where the egg will go.

5. Preheat the oven to 375°F.

6. In a small bowl, whisk together 1 egg and the water. Use a pastry brush to brush the egg wash over the dough. Freeze for 10 minutes before baking.

7. Crack the remaining egg into the indentation. Bake for 20 to 25 minutes, or until the egg white has completely cooked. Serve immediately.

**Tip:** Bacon would be a great addition to this galette. Dice 4 strips of bacon and cook to render off the fat. Add the bacon to the spinach mixture before layering the fillings in the galette.

# Day-After-Thanksgiving Turkey Pot Pie

No one ever eats all the turkey on Thanksgiving, and this is a great way to use leftovers. If you don't happen to have any cranberry sauce left over, buy a can of the whole-berry stuff.

Makes 1
(9-inch) pot pie

Prep time:
45 minutes, plus
1 hour to chill and
30 minutes to cool

Bake time:
1 hour 40 minutes

**For the filling**

4 tablespoons (½ stick) unsalted butter

1 cup diced celery

1 cup diced onion

1 cup diced carrot

1 tablespoon chopped fresh rosemary leaves

1 teaspoon salt

½ teaspoon freshly ground black pepper

2 cups shredded leftover cooked turkey

⅓ cup all-purpose flour

2 cups chicken broth or turkey broth

1 cup leftover cranberry sauce or store-bought whole-berry sauce

**For the crust**

Nonstick baking spray

1 large egg

1 tablespoon water

Double batch All-Butter Crust (page 22)

Flour, for dusting

1. **Make the filling:** In a large skillet over medium-high heat, melt the butter. Add the celery, onion, and carrot and stir to evenly coat in the butter. Add the rosemary, salt, and pepper. Cook for 8 to 10 minutes, stirring occasionally, until the vegetables are soft and translucent. Add the turkey and flour and stir until the mixture is evenly coated in the flour. Stir in the chicken broth, ½ cup at a time, and continue to cook, stirring, for about 5 more minutes until the mixture starts to thicken. Transfer the filling to a large bowl and refrigerate for 1 hour, until completely cool.

continues

2. Preheat the oven to 350°F. Lightly coat a 9-inch pie dish with baking spray. In a small bowl, whisk together the egg and water. Set aside.

3. **Roll out the crust:** Unwrap one dough disk onto a lightly floured work surface. Lightly flour a rolling pin and begin rolling the dough from the center outward. Turn the dough 90 degrees and roll again. Continue to turn and roll until you have a roughly 16-inch circle. Roll the dough onto the rolling pin, then unroll it onto the prepared pie dish. Press the dough lightly around the edge and into every crevice so the pie dough fills the dish. Let the edge of the dough hang off for now.

4. Spoon the cranberry sauce evenly over the bottom of the pie. Pour the turkey filling over the cranberry sauce. Do not mix. Using a pastry brush, brush the egg wash over the edge of the dough in the pie dish.

5. **Roll out the top crust:** Unwrap the second dough disk and roll out the dough into a 16-inch circle. Roll the dough onto the rolling pin, then unroll it over the filling. Trim the edge of the dough to hang ½ inch over the edge of the pie dish. Fold the dough under to seal and crimp.

6. Brush the egg wash over the crust. Cut an "X" into the center of the dough and 4 to 6 slits near the edge of the pie for vents. Place the dish in the freezer for 10 minutes.

7. Bake for 1 hour 40 minutes, or until the filling is bubbling and the crust is evenly golden.

8. Cool on a wire rack at room temperature for 30 minutes before serving.

**Tip:** You can easily make mini pot pies in ramekins. Halve the measurements of the crust and filling ingredients. Prepare the crust. Cook the filling over medium heat until thickened; cool completely in the refrigerator. Roll the crust into a 16-inch circle and use a 4-inch round cookie cutter to cut 4 circles. Grease 4 small ramekins with nonstick baking spray. Spoon cranberry sauce into the bottom of each ramekin, and then top with the turkey filling. Brush the edge of each ramekin with egg wash and adhere a top crust to each one. Brush the tops with egg wash and cut a circle to vent. Freeze for 10 minutes; bake in a preheated 425°F oven for 20 minutes, or until bubbly and golden brown.

# Chicken Pot Pie

**Serves 6**

**Prep time:**
20 minutes, plus
10 minutes to cool

**Bake time:**
35 minutes

A delightful comfort food classic, this recipe comes together quickly with the help of cooked chicken, frozen vegetables, and frozen phyllo dough. Use a pea, carrot, and green bean blend—it's a great combination in a pot pie. Try tossing the onion and celery in a food processor instead of chopping by hand to speed things up quite a bit.

1¾ cups chicken stock or broth
⅔ cup milk
⅓ cup all-purpose flour
1 tablespoon Italian seasoning
½ teaspoon salt
½ teaspoon poultry seasoning
¼ teaspoon freshly ground
   black pepper
1 cup finely chopped celery

½ cup finely chopped onion
2 garlic cloves, minced
3 cups diced cooked chicken
1 (12-ounce) bag frozen mixed
   vegetables
6 (9-by-14-inch) frozen phyllo
   dough sheets, thawed
Nonstick cooking spray

1. Preheat the oven to 375°F.

2. In a large oven-safe Dutch oven over medium-high heat, whisk the chicken stock, milk, flour, Italian seasoning, salt, poultry seasoning, and pepper until blended, and bring to a simmer. Reduce the heat so the mixture is gently cooking; stir in the celery, onion, and garlic and cook for 4 to 6 minutes, stirring constantly, until thickened. Add the chicken and mixed vegetables and stir well. Remove the pot from the heat.

3. Place 1 phyllo sheet on a large work surface and lightly spray it with cooking spray. Place another phyllo sheet over the first and spray it with cooking spray. Repeat with the remaining phyllo sheets. Place the layered phyllo sheets over the chicken and vegetable mixture.

4. Put the Dutch oven on a sturdy baking sheet and put the baking sheet in the oven. Bake for 30 to 35 minutes, or until the top is golden brown and the mixture is bubbly. Let cool for 10 minutes before serving.

**Tip:** If you've never worked with phyllo before, this is a great way to start! Its crispy, crackly texture makes a delicious contrast to the creamy, luxurious filling. To thaw phyllo, place it in the fridge overnight, and be sure to keep any unused portion covered with a kitchen towel as you work. This will keep it from drying out and cracking.

# Mini Quiches Lorraine

Anytime you're looking for a way to spice up breakfast or serve something elegant for brunch, give this quiche a try. It's also perfect on those breakfast-for-dinner nights—always a favorite! Quiche Lorraine is typically made with bacon and cheese, but you can pretty much add whatever meats and vegetables you'd like.

1 All-Butter Crust (page 22) or
   Gluten-Free Crust (page 24)
Flour, for dusting
6 thick-cut bacon slices, cut into
   small pieces
3 large eggs
⅔ cup heavy (whipping) cream

⅓ cup whole milk
¼ teaspoon freshly ground
   black pepper
Pinch salt
Pinch ground nutmeg
½ cup grated Gruyère cheese
¼ cup grated parmesan cheese

1. Line a baking sheet with parchment paper.

2. Roll out the dough on a lightly floured work surface to about ⅛ inch thick. Cut the dough into 4 (5-inch) circles. Line 4 (4-inch) tartlet pans with the dough, using a paring knife to trim off the excess, and place on the prepared baking sheet. Refrigerate for at least 10 minutes.

3. Preheat the oven to 350°F. Prick the bottoms of the tartlet shells with a fork in several spots. Be careful not to puncture the dough too much or the egg filling will seep through.

4. Blind bake the tartlet shells for 8 to 10 minutes, or until lightly browned. Set aside to cool. Lower the oven temperature to 250°F.

5. Line a plate with paper towels. In a small skillet over medium heat, cook the bacon until the fat is rendered and the bacon is lightly browned, 6 to 8 minutes. Transfer the bacon to the paper-towel-lined plate and set aside to cool.

6. In a medium bowl, whisk together the eggs, cream, milk, pepper, salt, and nutmeg.

7. Scatter the bacon equally among the tart shells. Sprinkle the Gruyère and parmesan equally among the tart shells, then pour the egg mixture into each shell.

8. Bake for 15 to 25 minutes or until the custard is set and a knife inserted in the middle comes out clean.

**Tip:** Be sure to bake immediately after filling with the egg mixture or the tart shells will start to soften.

# Tomato Tart with Burrata

With its delicious mozzarella-esque exterior and dreamy, creamy center, burrata classes up any dish. Here, it's combined with the bright taste of roasted tomatoes—a savory, flavorful, and beautiful snack that is much simpler than you might think.

Serves 4

Prep time:
5 minutes

Bake time:
20 minutes

1 tomato, thinly sliced

1 sheet frozen puff pastry, thawed

¼ cup pesto

1 tablespoon extra-virgin olive oil

Sea salt

Freshly ground black pepper

1 (4-ounce) piece burrata

8 fresh basil leaves

1. Preheat the oven to 400°F. Line a baking sheet with parchment paper.

2. Line a plate with a paper towel and arrange the tomato slices on the plate in a single layer. Place another paper towel on top to absorb liquid from both sides.

3. Unfold the puff pastry and lay it on the prepared baking sheet. Spread the pesto evenly atop the puff pastry, leaving a small border along the edges. Top with the tomato slices, making sure that none of the pieces overlap. Lightly drizzle the olive oil over the tomatoes and season with salt and pepper.

4. Bake for 20 minutes or until the puff pastry rises and is golden brown along the edges.

5. Remove the tart from the oven. Cut the burrata into several pieces and spread over the tart. Arrange the basil leaves on top and serve.

# Spinach and Swiss Quiche

Makes 1
(9-inch) quiche

Prep time:
10 minutes,
plus 30 minutes
to chill and
20 minutes to cool

Bake time:
1 hour 5 minutes

There are lots of kinds of quiche out there, but people keep coming back to this one—and for good reason. If you can find it, sub in Gruyère cheese for the Swiss, or chopped ham for the bacon.

1 All-Butter Crust (page 22) or
    Gluten-Free Crust (page 24)
Flour, for dusting
5 large eggs, at room temperature
½ cup whole milk
½ cup heavy (whipping) cream
½ teaspoon salt

½ teaspoon freshly ground
    black pepper
1 (10-ounce) box frozen spinach,
    thawed and water squeezed out
1 shallot, diced
1½ cups shredded Swiss
    cheese, divided

1. **Roll out the crust:** Unwrap the dough onto a lightly floured work surface. Lightly flour a rolling pin and begin rolling the dough from the center outward. Turn the dough 90 degrees and roll again. Continue to turn and roll until you have a roughly 16-inch circle. Roll the dough onto the rolling pin, then unroll it onto a 9-inch pie dish, leaving a 1-inch overhang around the edge. Trim off any excess dough. Fold the overhang underneath itself around the edge, crimping as you go. Refrigerate for 30 minutes.

2. Preheat the oven to 400°F.

3. Line the dough with parchment paper or aluminum foil and fill with dried beans or rice. Bake for about 15 minutes or until the edge begins to brown. Remove the parchment and weights. Prick the crust with a fork. Bake for about 7 minutes more or until the bottom crust is golden brown. Remove from the oven and let cool. Lower the oven temperature to 375°F.

4. **Make the filling:** In a large bowl, whisk together the eggs, milk, cream, salt, and pepper.

5. Layer the spinach, shallot, and 1 cup of cheese on the bottom crust. Pour in the egg mixture. Top with the remaining ½ cup of cheese.

6. Bake for 40 to 45 minutes, or until the center is set. The quiche may bubble up but will flatten as it cools. Let cool for 15 to 20 minutes before serving.

# Summer Vegetable Tart

Makes 1
(9-inch) tart

Prep time:
45 minutes, plus
1 hour to chill

Bake time:
1 hour

Fresh herbs and creamy goat cheese help show off summer squash and zucchini, making this a perfect warm-weather centerpiece for your meal.

**For the crust**

1 large egg yolk, at room temperature

2 tablespoons ice water

1¼ cups all-purpose flour

½ teaspoon salt

8 tablespoons (1 stick) cold unsalted butter, cut into cubes, plus additional room temperature butter to grease the pan

Flour, for dusting

**For the filling**

4 ounces soft goat cheese

1 teaspoon freshly squeezed lemon juice

1 teaspoon garlic powder

Salt

Freshly ground black pepper

1 zucchini, cut into ¼-inch slices

1 yellow squash, cut into ¼-inch slices

1 tablespoon olive oil

1 tablespoon minced fresh assorted herbs, such as thyme, parsley, chives, or rosemary

1. **Make the crust:** In a small bowl, mix together the egg yolk and water and set aside. In a large bowl, combine the flour and salt. Cut in the butter until the texture resembles coarse cornmeal. Add the egg mixture and mix with a fork until the dough begins to pull together. Turn the dough out onto a sheet of plastic wrap and flatten it into a 4-inch disk. Tightly wrap it and refrigerate for 30 minutes.

2. Unwrap the dough onto a lightly floured work surface. Lightly flour a rolling pin and roll out the dough until it is about ⅛ inch thick.

3.  Butter a 9-inch tart pan. Transfer the dough to the pan. Trim the edge. Loosely wrap the pan in plastic wrap and chill for 30 minutes more.

4.  **Make the filling:** While the crust chills, mix together the goat cheese, lemon juice, and garlic powder in a small bowl. Season with salt and pepper. Arrange the zucchini and squash between layers of paper towels and press down to absorb excess water.

5.  Preheat the oven to 375°F.

6.  Line the dough with parchment paper or aluminum foil. Fill with pie weights or dried beans. Bake for 5 to 10 minutes or until the edge begins to brown. Remove the parchment paper and the weights. Prick the crust with a fork. Bake for 5 minutes more or until the bottom looks dry (and no longer raw). Lower the oven temperature to 350°F.

7.  Spread the goat cheese mixture in the tart shell in an even layer. Arrange the zucchini and squash in an alternating pattern, slightly overlapping. Brush the vegetables with the oil. Sprinkle the herbs over the vegetables and season with salt and pepper. Bake for 40 to 45 minutes or until the vegetables are tender and cooked through.

# Mushroom Quiche

This hearty quiche is full of mushrooms and cheese, with a little bit of red pepper for color and flavor. Any type of mushroom will work here, from common button mushrooms to wild mushroom blends, so feel free to mix it up.

**Prep time:**
25 minutes,
plus 30 minutes
to chill and
20 minutes to cool

**Bake time:**
1 hour 10 minutes

1 All-Butter Crust (page 22) or
   Gluten-Free Crust (page 24)
Flour, for dusting
1 tablespoon olive oil
½ cup diced onion
3 cups sliced mushrooms
¼ cup diced red bell pepper
4 large eggs, at room temperature

½ cup milk
½ cup sour cream
½ teaspoon salt
½ teaspoon freshly ground
   black pepper
1½ cups shredded Cheddar
   cheese, divided

1. **Roll out the dough:** Unwrap the pie dough onto a lightly floured work surface. Lightly flour a rolling pin and begin rolling the dough from the center outward. Turn the dough 90 degrees and roll again. Continue to turn and roll until you have a roughly 16-inch circle. Roll the dough onto the rolling pin, then unroll it onto a 9-inch pie dish, leaving a 1-inch overhang around the edge. Trim off any excess dough. Fold the overhang underneath itself around the edge, crimping as you go. Refrigerate for 30 minutes.

2. Preheat the oven to 400°F. Line the dough with parchment paper or aluminum foil. Fill with dried beans or rice. Bake for about 15 minutes or until the edge begins to brown. Remove the parchment and weights. Prick the crust with a fork. Bake for about 7 minutes more or until the bottom crust is golden brown. Remove from the oven and let cool. Lower the oven temperature to 375°F.

3. **Make the filling:** In a large skillet, heat the oil over medium heat. Once hot, add the onion, mushrooms, and bell pepper and sauté until cooked, 5 to 7 minutes.

4. In a medium bowl, whisk together the eggs, milk, sour cream, salt, and pepper.

5. Layer the mushroom mixture and 1 cup of cheese on the bottom crust. Pour in the egg mixture. Top with the remaining ½ cup of cheese.

6. Bake for 40 to 45 minutes or until the center is set. About halfway through baking, check the crust; if it's browning too quickly you may want to tent the edge with foil. The quiche may bubble up but will flatten as it cools. Let cool for 15 to 20 minutes.

Toasted
S'mores
Icebox Pie
page 123

# Beyond Pies

# Rainbow Sprinkle Birthday Cake Hand Pies

**Makes 14 hand pies**

**Prep time:**
30 minutes, plus
10 minutes to freeze
and 1 hour to set

**Bake time:**
25 minutes

The filling in this recipe is an interpretation of the ultimate birthday cake flavor: funfetti. These hand pies are uber-playful, and let's be honest, anytime you can go wild with rainbow sprinkles is a good day.

**For the filling**

1 cup white chocolate chips

2 (8-ounce) packages cream cheese, at room temperature

¼ cup granulated sugar

4 large egg yolks

1 teaspoon rainbow sprinkles

**For the crust**

1 large egg

2 tablespoons water

Double batch All-Butter Crust (page 22) or Gluten-Free Crust (page 24)

**For the frosting**

1 cup powdered sugar

1 tablespoon milk

2 teaspoons corn syrup

Rainbow sprinkles, to garnish

1. **Make the filling:** In a microwave-safe bowl, microwave the white chocolate in 30-second increments, stirring between increments, until fully melted. In a stand mixer fitted with a paddle attachment, beat the cream cheese. Add the melted white chocolate and sugar and mix again, scraping down the sides as needed. Add the egg yolks and mix well. Fold in the sprinkles by hand and transfer to a piping bag.

2. Preheat the oven to 350°F. Line a baking sheet with parchment paper. In a small bowl, whisk together the egg and water. Set aside.

3. **Roll out the crust:** Unwrap the dough onto a lightly floured work surface. Lightly flour a rolling pin and roll out the dough from the center outward until ⅛ inch thick. Use a ruler and a knife or pizza cutter to cut out as many 2-by-3-inch rectangles as possible.

4. Place half the rectangles about 1 inch apart from each other on the prepared baking sheet. Brush the edges of each rectangle with egg wash. Pipe roughly 2 tablespoons of filling inside each rectangle, leaving a clear ½-inch border. Cover each with another rectangle and seal with a fork all around. Brush each hand pie with more egg wash. Freeze for 10 minutes.

5. Use a knife to poke 2 holes on top of each hand pie to vent. Bake for 24 minutes. Cool to room temperature.

6. **Make the frosting:** In a medium bowl, whisk together the powdered sugar, milk, and corn syrup. Use a spoon to smooth a dollop of frosting over each hand pie. Garnish with rainbow sprinkles and let the frosting set at room temperature for 1 hour before serving.

**Tip:** If you want to spruce up the white frosting, try adding some food gel to it. Just add it while you're mixing the frosting. You can even divide the frosting into separate bowls to make multiple colors for decorating the pies.

# Cannoli Cream–Filled Mini Tartlets

**Makes 24 mini tartlets**

**Prep time:**
20 minutes, plus
30 minutes to chill

**Bake time:**
15 minutes

Cannoli—delicate fried tubes of pastry dough filled with a sweetened ricotta cream cheese often studded with dried fruit or bits of chocolate—are a rare and special treat, because making them is laborious. These sweet tartlets filled with cannoli cream are a fine substitute. They have all the irresistible flavor of real Italian bakery cannoli, but they're a breeze to make.

All-purpose flour, for dusting
1 All-Butter Crust (page 22) or
   Gluten-Free Crust (page 24)
12 ounces whole-milk ricotta
   cheese, drained

8 ounces mascarpone cheese
½ cup plus 2 tablespoons powdered
   sugar, plus more for dusting
½ cup mini semisweet chocolate chips

1. Preheat the oven to 400°F.

2. Unwrap the dough on a lightly floured surface and roll out until ⅛ inch thick. Using a 2½-inch round cookie cutter, cut out 24 dough circles, gathering and rerolling the dough as necessary. Fit the dough circles into the cups of a mini muffin tin, pressing them in to form little dough cups.

3. Bake the crusts for 11 to 13 minutes, until lightly golden brown. Transfer the cups to a wire rack to cool completely.

4. While the cups cool, use a rubber spatula to mix together the ricotta and mascarpone cheeses in a large bowl until well combined and smooth. Add the powdered sugar and mix well. Add the chocolate chips and mix well. Cover and refrigerate for at least 30 minutes.

5. When ready to fill the cups, transfer the filling to a piping bag or a resealable plastic bag with the tip cut off one bottom corner. Pipe the filling into the pastry cups.

6. Dust with powdered sugar and serve. Cover and refrigerate any leftovers for up to 3 days.

**Tip:** Instead of piping the filling into the cups, use a large cookie scoop to fill them.

# Mudslide Ice Cream Pie

Makes 1 (9-inch) pie

Prep time:
30 minutes, plus
5 hours 45 minutes
to chill

Bake time:
10 minutes

Cool off with this refreshing dessert that has an ice cream base in a cookie crumb crust and is topped with pecans, fudge, and whipped cream. Coffee ice cream is a crowd-pleaser, but you can use any ice cream flavor you choose.

**1 unbaked Cookie Crust (page 33), made with chocolate sandwich cookies, pressed into a 9-inch pie dish**

**For the fudge sauce**

**4 ounces unsweetened chocolate, chopped**

**½ cup packed brown sugar**

**¼ cup granulated sugar**

**¾ cup plus 1 tablespoon heavy (whipping) cream**

**¼ cup light corn syrup**

**2 tablespoons unsalted butter**

**2 teaspoons vanilla extract**

**For the filling**

**2 pints coffee ice cream**

**½ cup chopped pecans**

**For the topping**

**1½ cups cold heavy (whipping) cream**

**¼ cup powdered sugar**

**1 teaspoon vanilla extract**

**½ cup chocolate syrup**

1. Preheat the oven to 350°F.

2. Bake the crust for 8 minutes. Let cool completely.

3. **Make the fudge sauce:** In a microwave-safe bowl, combine the chocolate, brown sugar, granulated sugar, cream, and corn syrup. Heat in the microwave in 30- to 60-second increments, stirring between increments, until the mixture is smooth, well combined, and thick. Whisk in the butter and vanilla.

4. Spoon half of the fudge sauce into the crust and spread it out in an even layer. Place the crust in the freezer for 15 minutes.

5. **Fill the pie:** Let the ice cream sit on the counter for about 10 minutes to soften. Spoon the softened ice cream into the crust and use a rubber spatula to smooth it into an even layer. Freeze for 30 minutes.

6. Spoon the remaining fudge sauce over the top. Sprinkle the pecans on top and freeze for 1 hour.

7. **Make the topping:** In a large bowl, combine the cream, powdered sugar, and vanilla and beat with an electric mixer until it holds stiff peaks. Top the pie with the whipped cream and return it to the freezer. Freeze for at least 4 hours.

8. Serve the pie chilled, drizzled with the chocolate syrup.

**Tip:** Try mint chip ice cream for more of a grasshopper pie.

# Toasted S'mores Icebox Pie

S'mores are the essence of summer. It's hard to find someone who doesn't have a fond memory of making them as a kid. The graham cracker crust has a hint of salt that brings out the sweetness in the pie. And remember, the more you broil or torch the marshmallow topping, the better it'll be. Drizzle the top of your pie with a homemade chocolate sauce for even more chocolatey goodness.

Makes 1 (9-inch) pie

Prep time:
25 minutes, plus
4 hours to chill

1½ cups bittersweet or semisweet chocolate chips

2 tablespoons unsweetened cocoa powder

⅛ teaspoon salt

⅓ cup hot water

1½ cups cold heavy (whipping) cream

1 Cookie Crust (page 33), made with graham crackers, pressed into a 9-inch pie dish and refrigerated for 10 minutes

20 large marshmallows

1. In a large microwave-safe bowl, microwave the chocolate chips in 30-second increments, stirring with a rubber spatula between increments, until fully melted.

2. In small bowl, whisk together the cocoa powder, salt, and hot water, then whisk it into the melted chocolate until thoroughly combined.

3. In the bowl of a stand mixer fitted with the whisk attachment, or in a large bowl and using a hand mixer, whip the heavy cream until stiff peaks form. Fold the whipped cream into the chocolate mixture until thoroughly combined.

continues

4. Pour the filling into the prepared crust. Refrigerate the pie for at least 4 hours.

5. Preheat the broiler. Just before serving, arrange the marshmallows over the top of the pie. Broil the pie for 1 minute to toast the marshmallows or use a kitchen torch to toast the marshmallows.

6. This pie is best served the day it's made. It can be stored, uncovered, in the refrigerator for up to 3 days, or wrapped in plastic and frozen for up to 1 month.

**Tip:** Want more chocolate in this pie? Swap the graham cracker crust for the Cookie Crust (page 33) made with chocolate sandwich cookies and prepare as instructed.

# Crustless Pear Custard Tart

This recipe has only six ingredients and takes only a few minutes to put together. You'll wonder how it can possibly be so good with such little effort. Here's the secret: you bake tender pears in a sweet, custardy batter. The result is sublime. Instead of making one big tart, you could make six individual ones in mini tart tins.

Makes 1
(9-inch) tart

Prep time:
10 minutes

Bake time:
25 minutes

¾ cup (1½ sticks) unsalted butter, plus more for preparing the dish
1½ cups powdered sugar, plus more for dusting
1 cup almond meal
⅓ cup all-purpose flour
3 large eggs, beaten
3 pears, cored and cut into wedges

1. Preheat the oven to 400°F. Lightly grease a 9-inch round tart pan with butter.

2. In a small saucepan over medium heat, melt the butter and cook for about 3 minutes until it just turns golden brown. Remove from the heat and let cool.

3. Meanwhile, in a medium bowl, stir together the powdered sugar, almond meal, and flour. Add the melted butter and the eggs and stir to mix well. Pour the batter into the pan and arrange the pear wedges on top.

4. Bake for 15 minutes, then lower the heat to 350°F. Bake for 5 to 10 minutes more, until just golden brown.

5. Dust with powdered sugar, slice into wedges, and serve warm or at room temperature.

# Mini Apple Pies with Crumb Topping

Bite-size desserts are a fun way to enjoy favorites. Here, apple pie gets a mini makeover with a sweet, buttery crumb topping. This is especially great for fall tailgating.

Makes 12 pies

Prep time:
15 minutes, plus
30 minutes to cool

Bake time:
20 minutes

1 refrigerated piecrust (from a package of 2)

2 apples, cored and diced

2 tablespoons granulated sugar

¼ cup, plus 1 tablespoon all-purpose flour, divided

1 teaspoon ground cinnamon

¼ cup packed light brown sugar

2 tablespoons unsalted butter, melted

1. Preheat the oven to 425°F.

2. Place the piecrust on a cutting board or work surface. Using a 4-inch round cookie or biscuit cutter, or other similar-size object, cut the dough into 12 rounds. Press them into the cups of a standard-size muffin tin. Continue until all the dough has been used. Gather and reroll the dough scraps for the last few rounds.

3. In a medium bowl, stir together the apples, granulated sugar, 1 tablespoon of flour, and the cinnamon until fully combined. Spoon the apple filling into the dough rounds.

4. In a small bowl, stir together the remaining ¼ cup of flour and the brown sugar. Drizzle in the melted butter and mix well. Spoon the topping over the pies.

5. Bake for 18 to 20 minutes or until golden on top.

6. Let the pies cool for 30 minutes in the tin before loosening them with a knife and transferring to a wire rack to cool completely.

# French-Style Apple Tart

Serves 6 to 8

Prep time:
40 minutes, plus
1 hour to chill and
30 minutes to cool

Bake time:
15 minutes

This style of deeply caramelized, upside-down apple tart is known as a tarte Tatin in France, where you'll find it on bistro menus and in bakeries across the country. The dish dates from the late 1800s and was first made by an innkeeper named Caroline Tatin. It looks fancy, but it's actually quite easy to make. Try preparing it with other fruits, such as pears, pineapples, or plums.

**For the dough**

2⅓ cups all-purpose flour, plus more for dusting

1 teaspoon baking powder

¾ teaspoon sea salt

1 cup (2 sticks) cold unsalted butter, cubed

¼ to ½ cup ice water, as needed

**For the apples**

¼ cup (½ stick) unsalted butter

¾ cup granulated sugar

8 Granny Smith apples, cored, peeled, and cut into ⅛-inch slices

Zest of 1 orange

Pinch ground cinnamon

Powdered sugar, for dusting

1. **Make the dough:** In a food processor, pulse the flour, baking powder, and salt together. Add the butter and pulse until the mixture looks like coarse cornmeal. With the motor running, add just enough ice water through the feed tube so that the dough forms into a loose ball. Gather the dough into a ball and cover it with plastic wrap. Let it rest for 1 hour or overnight in the refrigerator.

2. Preheat the oven to 500°F.

3. **Prepare the apples:** In a large, oven-safe, heavy skillet over medium heat, melt the butter until foamy. Add the sugar and cook, stirring occasionally, until it starts to caramelize and turn light brown, about 5 minutes. Stir in the apples, orange zest, and cinnamon until the apples are well coated. Cook, stirring occasionally, until the apples start to brown, about 10 minutes. Remove from the heat and arrange the apple slices in circles in the skillet.

4. Unwrap the dough onto a lightly floured work surface. Lightly flour a rolling pin and begin rolling the dough from the center outward. Turn the dough 90 degrees and roll again. Continue to turn and roll until you have a 12-inch circle. Top the apples with the dough, tucking the edge in around the side of the skillet.

5. Bake until the crust is golden brown, 10 to 15 minutes.

6. Let it cool for 20 to 30 minutes. Flip the tart over onto a serving plate, dust with powdered sugar, and serve immediately.

**Tip:** Be careful not to overmix the dough, or else the crust will be tough. Gluten acts like a muscle—the more you work it, the harder it gets. Similarly, when you let the dough rest, it will become softer.

# Lemon Tart

This is a simple home version of a bakery classic. The lemon flavor is very refreshing, especially after a rich meal.

Makes 1
(9-inch) tart

Prep time:
20 minutes, plus
2 hours 30 minutes
to chill

Bake time:
45 minutes

**For the dough**

½ cup powdered sugar

¼ cup (½ stick) unsalted butter, at room temperature

1 teaspoon vanilla extract

3 large egg yolks

1¼ cups all-purpose flour

**For the filling**

3 large eggs

3 large egg yolks

⅔ cup granulated sugar

½ cup freshly squeezed lemon juice (from about 3 lemons)

Zest of 2 lemons

3 tablespoons unsalted butter, melted

Pinch sea salt

**For topping (optional)**

Fresh berries

Powdered sugar

1. **Make the dough:** In a food processor, combine the powdered sugar, butter, and vanilla and process until well mixed. Add the egg yolks and process until blended. Add the flour and pulse several times. Do not worry if the dough does not form a ball. Gather the dough into a ball and cover it with plastic wrap. Refrigerate for at least 2 hours or, even better, overnight.

2. Unwrap the dough onto a lightly floured work surface. Lightly flour a rolling pin, and roll out the dough into an 11-inch circle about ⅛ inch thick. Roll the dough onto the rolling pin, then unroll it onto a 9-inch tart pan. Gently press the dough into the corners, leaving a ¼-inch overhang around the edges. Crimp the edge tightly, and then refrigerate for 30 minutes.

continues

3. Preheat the oven to 375°F.

4. Bake the tart shell until very lightly browned, about 10 minutes.

5. **Make the filling:** In a medium bowl, whisk together all the ingredients for the filling until smooth. Pour the filling into the tart shell.

6. Bake until just set, 30 to 35 minutes. Cool on a wire rack to room temperature.

7. **To top the pie:** Arrange fresh berries on top, and dust with powdered sugar just before serving.

# Mixed Berry Hand Pies

Who doesn't love a cute little pie you can hold in your hand? These are super fun to make, and once you get to know the recipe, you can play around with the fillings.

1 tablespoon cornstarch

1 tablespoon water

16 ounces fresh or frozen mixed berries

½ cup granulated sugar

1 tablespoon freshly squeezed lemon juice

½ teaspoon vanilla extract

¼ teaspoon salt

¼ teaspoon ground cinnamon

All-purpose flour, for dusting

1 All-Butter Crust (page 22) or Gluten-Free Crust (page 24)

1 large egg, beaten

Turbinado sugar, for topping

Makes 6 to
8 hand pies

Prep time:
30 minutes, plus
30 minutes to chill

Bake time:
35 minutes

1. Line a baking sheet with parchment paper.

2. In a small bowl, mix together the cornstarch and water until smooth. Set aside.

3. In a medium saucepan over medium heat, mix together the berries, sugar, lemon juice, vanilla, salt, and cinnamon, and cook until the berries begin to break down a bit and release their juices, 4 to 6 minutes. Add the cornstarch mixture and cook, stirring often, until the mixture comes to a boil. Remove from the heat and let the mixture cool completely. It will continue to thicken as it cools.

4. Unwrap the dough onto a lightly floured work surface. Lightly flour a rolling pin and begin rolling the dough from the center outward until it is about ⅛ inch thick. Using a round cookie cutter or the shape of your choice, cut out as many shapes as you can, making sure there are two pieces for each hand pie. You should have between 12 and 16 pieces.

continues

5. Place half of the dough circles on the prepared baking sheet. Spoon 2 to 3 tablespoons of filling onto the center of each. Place another dough circle on top and, using a fork, crimp the edges closed. With a sharp knife, cut 3 slits on the top of each pie. Brush the egg wash on each pie and sprinkle with turbinado sugar. Refrigerate for up to 30 minutes.

6. Preheat the oven to 375°F.

7. Bake for 30 to 35 minutes or until golden brown. Let cool on the baking sheet until the pies are cool enough to handle.

8. Store the pies in an airtight container in the refrigerator for up to 3 days. To reheat, place them in a 350°F oven for 5 minutes. They also taste great cold or at room temperature.

# Fresh Fruit Tartlets with Pastry Cream

**Makes 12 tartlets**

**Prep time:**
30 minutes, plus
2 hours to chill

**Bake time:**
15 minutes

Here, a store-bought piecrust saves the day, helping these tartlets come together with very little hands-on time. (Of course, if you feel moved, use the All-Butter Crust on page 22!) These tartlets are great topped with mixed berries, sliced stone fruits such as peaches or nectarines, or pears. Their small size and colorful topping possibilities make them a great dessert for any celebratory event.

All-purpose flour, for dusting
1 uncooked 9-inch piecrust (homemade or store-bought)
4 large egg yolks
½ cup granulated sugar
¼ cup cornstarch
Pinch salt

2 cups low-fat or whole milk
1½ teaspoons vanilla extract
Fresh fruit, for topping the tartlets (sliced peaches, nectarines, strawberries, raspberries, blueberries, or other fruit as desired)

1. Preheat the oven to 400°F.

2. Unwrap the dough onto a lightly floured work surface. Lightly flour a rolling pin and begin rolling the dough from the center outward until it is ⅛ inch thick. Using a 3½-inch round cookie cutter, cut out 12 dough circles. Fit the dough circles into the cups of a standard-size muffin tin, pressing them in to form little dough cups.

3. Bake for 11 to 13 minutes until lightly golden brown. Let cool completely.

4. While the cups cool, in a medium bowl, whisk the egg yolks until smooth.

5. In a saucepan set over medium heat, combine the sugar, cornstarch, and salt. Whisking continuously, add the milk in a slow, steady stream. Cook for about 5 minutes, whisking, until the mixture bubbles and thickens.

6. While whisking constantly, ladle about one-third of the milk mixture into the egg yolks. Transfer the egg yolk mixture to the saucepan, still whisking constantly, and bring to a boil. Cook for 2 to 4 minutes, whisking, until the mixture is very thick. Remove the saucepan from the heat and stir in the vanilla. Transfer the pastry cream to a bowl, cover with plastic wrap, and refrigerate for 2 hours.

7. Spoon, pipe, or scoop the pastry cream into the tart shells. Top with fresh fruit and serve immediately.

**Tip:** For especially pretty tartlets, use a scalloped cookie cutter. The edges will be turned up when you press the dough into the muffin tin, giving your tartlets a pretty finished edge.

# No-Bake Strawberry Cream Pie

Makes 1 (9-inch) pie

Prep time:
20 minutes, plus
5 hours to chill

When strawberry season rolls around, there is nothing better than combining those sweet berries with a creamy no-bake pie filling set in a shortbread cookie crumb crust. Mascarpone is a soft, mild Italian cheese made with cream, giving it a high fat content and a luxurious mouthfeel. If you can't find it, substitute a good full-fat ricotta cheese.

**For the crust**

2¾ cups (about 11 ounces) crushed shortbread cookie crumbs
1 tablespoon granulated sugar

6 tablespoons (¾ stick) unsalted butter, melted

**For the filling**

1½ cups sliced fresh strawberries
2 tablespoons granulated sugar
¾ cup mascarpone cheese, at room temperature

¾ cup plain Greek yogurt, at room temperature
¼ cup plus 2 tablespoons powdered sugar

1. **Make the crust:** In a medium bowl, stir together the cookie crumbs, sugar, and butter until thoroughly combined and beginning to clump. Press the mixture into the bottom and up the sides of a 9-inch pie dish, pressing firmly. Freeze for 1 hour.

2. **Make the filling:** When the crust is frozen, put the strawberries in a medium bowl and toss with the sugar. Let the strawberries sit to macerate for 15 minutes.

3. While the strawberries sit, combine the mascarpone, yogurt, and powdered sugar in another medium bowl. Spread half the mixture in an even layer on top of the crust.

4. Layer half the strawberries on top and cover them with the remaining mascarpone-yogurt mixture. Arrange the remaining strawberries on top.

5. Refrigerate for at least 4 hours before slicing and serving.

**Tip:** If you want to shorten the waiting time, bake the crust in a 350°F oven for about 8 minutes instead of freezing it for 1 hour.

Mini
Apple Pies
with Crumb
Topping
page 127

| VOLUME EQUIVALENTS | U.S. Standard | U.S. Standard (ounces) | Metric (approximate) |
|---|---|---|---|
| **LIQUID** | 2 tablespoons | 1 fl. oz. | 30 mL |
| | ¼ cup | 2 fl. oz. | 60 mL |
| | ½ cup | 4 fl. oz. | 120 mL |
| | 1 cup | 8 fl. oz. | 240 mL |
| | 1½ cups | 12 fl. oz. | 355 mL |
| | 2 cups or 1 pint | 16 fl. oz. | 475 mL |
| | 4 cups or 1 quart | 32 fl. oz. | 1 L |
| | 1 gallon | 128 fl. oz. | 4 L |
| **DRY** | ⅛ teaspoon | — | 0.5 mL |
| | ¼ teaspoon | — | 1 mL |
| | ½ teaspoon | — | 2 mL |
| | ¾ teaspoon | — | 4 mL |
| | 1 teaspoon | — | 5 mL |
| | 1 tablespoon | — | 15 mL |
| | ¼ cup | — | 59 mL |
| | ⅓ cup | — | 79 mL |
| | ½ cup | — | 118 mL |
| | ⅔ cup | — | 156 mL |
| | ¾ cup | — | 177 mL |
| | 1 cup | — | 235 mL |
| | 2 cups or 1 pint | — | 475 mL |
| | 3 cups | — | 700 mL |
| | 4 cups or 1 quart | — | 1 L |
| | ½ gallon | — | 2 L |
| | 1 gallon | — | 4 L |

**OVEN TEMPERATURES**

| Fahrenheit | Celsius (approximate) |
|---|---|
| 250°F | 120°C |
| 300°F | 150°C |
| 325°F | 165°C |
| 350°F | 180°C |
| 375°F | 190°C |
| 400°F | 200°C |
| 425°F | 220°C |
| 450°F | 230°C |

**WEIGHT EQUIVALENTS**

| U.S. Standard | Metric (approximate) |
|---|---|
| ½ ounce | 15 g |
| 1 ounce | 30 g |
| 2 ounces | 60 g |
| 4 ounces | 115 g |
| 8 ounces | 225 g |
| 12 ounces | 340 g |
| 16 ounces or 1 pound | 455 g |

# Index

## Acknowledgments

To Callisto Media, thank you for the opportunity to share my recipes with the world. To my editor, Cecily, thank you for your guidance.

To my husband, as corny as it sounds, you're my rock. You're my favorite person to do life with. Thank you for not judging me when I destroyed the oven several times. Thank you for tasting every dessert, even when you didn't want to. And thank you for cleaning mountains of dishes.

To my mom and dad, your love and encouragement are why I am who I am today. I am forever grateful to you both.

To my KTRG family, I've learned so much over the years from each one of you. Thank you.

## About the Authors

 **Saura Kline** is a professional pastry chef, dessert blogger, and cookbook author. Saura grew up in Los Angeles and has been cooking in professional kitchen settings for more than 10 years. Originally drawn to wedding cakes, she found her passion creating restaurant-quality desserts. She now lives with her husband and their bull terrier in Denver, where she is currently a pastry chef. Saura has contributed as a recipe developer for Yummly. You can find her recipes on the website or app.

Saura has a dessert blog, *Sweet Saura* (SweetSaura.com), where she shares her favorite recipes with dessert lovers. She is the author of three cookbooks: *Easy as Pie*, *Pies That Inspire*, and *Small Batch Baking Cookbook*.

Other contributors to this book include **Robin Donovan** and **Heather Perine**.

CPSIA information can be obtained
at www.ICGtesting.com
Printed in the USA
JSHW032307310821
18316JS00001B/4